COLLINS POCKET REFERENCE

SCOTTISH
MYTHS & CUSTOMS

C. Shaw

Illustrations by
David Braysher

D1388412

HarperCollins*Publishers*

HarperCollins Publishers
P O Box, Glasgow G4 0NB

First published 1997

ISBN 0 00 472114 4

Reprint 10 9 8 7 6 5 4 3 2 1

A catalogue record for this book
is available from the British Library

Distributed in the United States by
Roberts Rinehart Publishers
6309 Monarch Park Place
Niwot
Colorado 80503

Printed and bound in Great Britain by Caledonian
International Book Manufacturing Ltd, Glasgow G64

Contents

Introduction

Customs, myths, legends and folklore, often dating from as far back as pre-historic times, help to make Scotland the country it is. From the Norse-inspired sea monsters of the extreme north to the legendary anvil weddings at Gretna Green on the English border, the stories and traditions that have lasted down to the twenty-first century have been shaped and guided by the experiences of the past.

Given its small population, Scotland is rich in folklore and folk tradition, and its continuation through the generations has relied heavily on the oral tradition that was central to the Scottish way of life for centuries, seen in the high respect given to the clan *Seannachie*, the story teller. It is a credit to these traditions that so many of the old customs are still so familiar today.

A sense of history and its development is brought forcibly home to anyone reading about custom and myth. Seeing how familiar beliefs and practices have evolved can give us a living link to the country's past, and shows how Scotland has developed into the country it is today. For example, the many ceremonies and festivals involving fire are a direct inheritance from the pagan Celts, led in sun-worship by the Druids almost 2000 years ago. The Christian missionaries who came to Scotland grafted their own festivals and ceremonies onto the already-existing pagan ones to persuade the natives to convert. In the northernmost islands, the Scandinavian influence exerted for centuries is also obvious in popular legends, passed on by generations of storytellers right up to the present.

Religion, too, has always been important in shaping the history and customs of Scotland, from the pre-Christians to the advent of Christianity through the Reformation of 1560 and its aftermath. Despite the suppression of Catholicism, Scotland's saints continued to be revered, and figure in many of the legends that have best survived the passage of time.

Customs surround all the rites of passage, in human lives as well in the passing of seasons and years. Many customs have changed or modified in modern times, and their original significance has been completely forgotten or is unknown to those following them. Some other customs have been forgotten entirely, while other new ones have emerged from modern beliefs and attitudes in very recent years. Examples of how popular beliefs and myths still make their presence felt daily in the lives of Scots can be found in just about any sphere of everyday life you care to examine. Popular Scottish myths and customs are also reflected in literature, from the ballad collections of Walter Scott to the poetry of Robert Burns.

The wealth and variety of material on offer throws up the problem of what to include in a book like this – or rather, what to omit. This book provides a general introduction to some of the more commonly practised customs and widely believed myths, while including a few important local variations. Sadly, much has had to be left out, particularly customs which are very local rather than national, or found at least over a wider area.

As ever-more rapid technological advances make the world smaller and more homogeneous, Scotland's cultural traditions will be influenced increasingly by ideas from further afield. Even maintaining the national customs that have survived so far will take effort and determination by future generations of Scots. We must hope they succeed – the country's cultural heritage would be less rich and much less special without them.

1: *Birth*

The arrival of a new child is one of the central life events for any prospective parent and, as with all such defining events, was surrounded with a forest of superstition, tradition and mythology which grew up around it through the centuries – some fearful, some helpful and a few downright sadistic.

Traditionally there were many birth rituals which had to be observed by an expectant mother nearing her 'crying', as labour was descriptively known. These have now almost completely died out in Scotland, partly because of the modern tendency towards hospital births, and partly because births do not happen so often in most families as they once did.

An average Scottish family now has between one and three children, but before the development of more reliable and widely available contraception in the 1960s, most women would have had many more. In hard economic terms, a large family was like money in the bank for the parents. It meant that even if some of the youngsters died – as they very well might, either in childbirth, from one of the many then-irresistible infectious diseases, or in war – others would survive to provide for their parents in old age – assuming that their mother had not herself already died in childbirth.

◆ The Confinement ◆ ◆

The days leading up to the birth and those just after it were considered to be fraught with danger – often with good reason, as the death rates among both mothers and their newborn babies were many times greater than now, even as relatively recently as in the early part of the twentieth century.

But it was not just mortal danger that was feared: women and their infants were particularly vulnerable to supernatural forces during birth, and all possible precautions were taken to protect them. Fairies were the worst threat, due to their fondness for human milk and their craving for unbaptised babies.

The Howdie

The mother-to-be's main attendant at this time was the 'howdie', an old Scots term meaning 'handy woman'. She was usually a local woman who acted as midwife for her neighbours and, just as importantly, instructed them in the rituals needed to keep both mother and baby safe from harm.

As soon as the first pains of labour began, the howdie would be summoned. One of her first and most pressing duties was untying all the knots on the mother's clothing and unlocking all the doors in the house. This symbolic act was thought to give the baby easier passage to the outside world.

Mirrors were covered or turned to the wall to protect the infant, whose soul might otherwise become imprisoned behind the glass. In some parts, a similar belief extended to bottles, which had to be left uncorked for fear of evil forces capturing the new baby's spirit in them.

Other Precautions

It was vital that no other pregnant woman should be in the room during labour. If an expectant mother went into labour while another pregnant woman was in the same house, they had to take steps to ensure that their babies were not confused and born to the wrong mother. This involved each woman holding one end of a stalk of grass or straw, which they then broke between them while repeating, 'Ye tak' yours and I'll tak' mine'.

Reflecting the ancient Celtic reverence for the sun and fire, many of Scotland's traditional customs display a belief in the protective properties of fire, and those surrounding childbirth are no exception. The howdie would pass a burning brand 'sunwise' (i.e. east-to-west) over or around the woman in labour to guard her from malign influences. A similar ceremony was often performed over the newly born child, or else it would be handed back and forth over a fire between the howdie and another of the women present.

During labour, the howdie would use various herbal concoctions to ease the expectant mother's pain. A number of these preparations included rowan berries. The red fruits of this sacred tree were credited with magical properties which gave protection against fairies and guarded both mother and baby against the evil eye, while a naturally occurring narcotic in the berries helped to relieve the labour pains.

In the Western Isles, pain relief was provided by a rare seed called the Virgin's Nut, called after the faint cross-marking on it. This was blessed and given to reduce pain and ensure a safe delivery.

Role of the Father

Very few birth customs in Scotland involved the father: indeed, until as late as the 1970s, the customary place for Scottish fathers-to-be was anywhere but in delivery room. Any male involvement in childbirth was minimal, and even a doctor (in those days, usually male) would be summoned only to a particularly difficult birth.

At most births, the father was represented only symbolically, by a pair of his trousers hanging over the foot of the bed. This was intended to represent his protection of his wife and their new child in his absence.

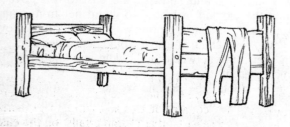

Symbolic representation of the new father at the birth bed

◆ The Baby ◆ ◆

After the Birth

Once the baby was born, it became the focus of the howdie's attention. She would immediately put a protective substance into its mouth to ward off the evil eye. This varied from area to area, although it was usually salt, whisky or butter.

Another preparation would then be made for the women present at the birth. A dish of oatmeal and water was passed among them, and each took three spoonfuls to endow the baby with strength and luck.

In common with other places, Scottish ritual dictated that the afterbirth should be buried, a task carried out by the howdie. Often a tree was planted by the site of the buried afterbirth, and its growth was interpreted as yet another omen of the child's future. A tall, straight tree meant that the child would become a healthy, strong adult; a leafless tree symbolised infertility and, most terrifying of all for the parents, a sickly tree indicated that the child would be weak and would suffer an early death.

To celebrate the health of the mother and child, a 'crying cheese' would be specially made in advance for the occasion. This was left untouched until after the baby was safely born, when it was cut by the howdie and divided among the women who had been present, washed down with ale. This exclusively female celebration had different names across the country: it was known as the 'merry meht' in the north-east, and as 'cummerfalls' on the east coast.

Later, the celebrations were also enjoyed by the male members of the family, whose responsibility it was to 'wet the baby's head' – celebrating its arrival with drink, usually whisky or beer. This was a practice that few found onerous, and it is one of a small number of birth customs that survives throughout Scotland to the present day.

◆ Birth Omens and Signs ◆ ◆

Whenever a child is born, its family naturally speculate on what the future may hold for it. Traditional thinking often went one step further, using and interpreting aspects of the birth and the new baby's behaviour to predict its future.

Timing

In Scotland, some significance was attached to the date of the birth: babies born on the first of the month were considered particularly lucky. Consequently, those born on the second of the month were less fortunate, as this was an inauspicious date, thought to signify second-best.

The day of the child's birth was also considered highly significant in many areas, as the traditional rhyme – not just known in Scotland – shows:

> Monday's child is fair of face,
> Tuesday's child is full of grace,
> Wednesday's child is full of woe,
> Thursday's child has far to go.
> Friday's child is loving and giving,

Saturday's child works hard for a living.
But the child that is born on the Sabbath Day
Is blithe and bonny and good and gay.

Position in the family could also be important. A seventh child of a seventh child, for example, was believed by many cultures to be endowed with second sight and healing powers.

The Caul

Second sight was also one of the special gifts credited to any child born with a caul. This membrane, very occasionally found fully or partially covering the head and face of a newly born baby, was a piece of the amniotic sac which had contained the baby in the womb. It was interpreted as a sign that the child was especially lucky or gifted, and was removed, dried and preserved, bringing good fortune to its owner and anyone who subsequently possessed it.

The caul protected the new baby from harm or theft by fairies. It was also a powerful charm against drowning, and dried cauls were highly prized by sailors, who often took them to sea to ward off a shipwreck.

Hanselling

'Hanselling' the new baby meant giving it a silver coin, and was thought to bring good luck to both the child and the giver. This custom was also thought to reveal the child's future attitude to money. A baby that grasped the coin and held it tightly would be miserly and penny-pinch-

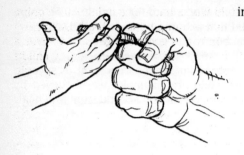

ing, while a child that quickly dropped it or lost the coin would go on to be a spendthrift. Hanselling is a custom which still continues to thrive in mod-ern-day Scotland although these days, probably in the interests of safety, the gift is more often left in the pram or cradle than handed directly to the child. However, it is still considered to bring good fortune to the donor and the recipient.

Protective Measures

As soon as the child was born, several precautions had to be taken to protect it. A changeling was a mother's worst fear (see p. 19), and was considered a very real danger until after the child was christened. There were numerous rituals to be seen to in the days between birth and bap-tism.

It was not wise to take a baby out of the room of its birth before christening time, because this risked tempting the fairies and any other malign forces who might want to harm the child. If such a move was absolutely necessary, it had to be done in a specific way.

The person carrying the unbaptised baby out of the

delivery room should take the child upstairs before going anywhere else. If this was not practical, they should carry it a few rungs up a ladder or even stand on a chair or a box. This elevation supposedly represented the child's future prosperity and well-being, so on no account should its first journey be downstairs.

It was also important to avoid talking about an unbaptised baby, and especially not to praise it: any praise of the child could attract the attention of fairies who were always keen to steal away the most attractive human children. Any unguarded comments made either to or about the child should be followed by a blessing, such as 'God save him/her'.

The wrath of God was also used as a reason to avoid praising a baby. Too many compliments for her child were thought likely to induce a mother to love it more than anything else. This, it was thought, would inevitably bring God's wrath down on them both. Several sad accounts exist of newly bereaved mothers being told that they should thank God for saving them from blasphemous pride in the child.

Water

In a custom in some ways reminiscent of the christening ceremony, new-born babies in parts of northern Scotland, including Inverness and Perth, were immediately immersed in cold water. Earliest reports describe plunging the child into a stream, although this later evolved into a basin of water.

Although the idea of taking a baby that had just left the warmth and safety of the womb and dipping it into cold

Immersing a newborn baby in cold water

water may sound sadistic, there were often practical reasons for the howdie's actions.

After a long or difficult birth, babies could be hesitant to take their first breath. The shock of touching the cold water could be all that was needed to encourage them to use their lungs. Conversely, it was also important that the water was not too cold: the baby's heart could simply stop if the shock of the freezing-cold water proved too much.

When the weather was too harsh or wet for such a ceremony – a common enough problem in Scotland – the baby's first bath would have been in front of a roaring fire, preferably of rowan or some other protective wood, with a piece of gold or silver in the water to symbolise future wealth. Given the chilly alternative for mother as well as child, this became the preferred option.

Changelings

The slightest slip in the vigilance of the mother or the howdie could be critical, as fairies would creep into the house and steal away the new baby at any chance they were given, leaving a changeling in its place.

Explanations for this theft varied across Scotland. In most areas it was believed that human children were coveted because they were stronger, and they were taken away to improve the fairy gene-pool. At the same time, the fairy left in exchange would also benefit from the human mother's milk. A more sinister explanation from the north east claimed that, every seven years, the fairies had to make a sacrifice to the Devil, and they would steal a human child rather than lose one of their own.

A changeling could take various forms: in Highland mythology it was sometimes a stock of wood, carved in the shape of a child and made to seem

Plotting to leave a changeling

19

alive by fairy magic. The appearance of life would last only a few days, when the 'child' would seem to die. Its grieving parents would bury the wood, never knowing their child's true fate. A changeling might also be thought to be a very old fairy who needed looking after. These were particularly cantankerous, constantly wailing and crying for food.

The most common changelings were sickly fairy children, placed with a human mother in order to thrive better on the coveted human milk. They tended to die young, with one report from the Northern Isles reporting a changeling's death after about 20 years. This shortened lifespan is confirmed by other reports. But by acting quickly, it was sometimes possible for the parents to retrieve their own child. One method was to take the changeling to a place where fairies gathered, and leave it there overnight with gifts of food. If these offerings were acceptable, the real child would be returned the next morning.

Not all suspect babies were so lucky. Some horrific and barbaric solutions to the perceived problem were devised, including throwing the child into a fire or placing it on a red-hot shovel. This would supposedly send the fairy flying up the chimney and ensure the real baby's return. In reality, this was the horrible fate of many perfectly normal children who were simply fretful, or who displayed some sign of physical or mental impairment.

Belief in changelings was by no means exclusive to Scotland, and accounts of them crop up in many other countries. In Germany, the reformer Martin Luther reported such fairy activity in 1541. Yet the idea seems to have been particularly widespread and enduring among the Scots, with reports of changelings being found in different parts of the country as recently as within the last century.

◆ The Baby's Surroundings ◆ ◆

The Cradle

As the place where the new baby would spend the greater part of its early days, the cradle was thought important enough to merit rituals of its own.

It was thought extremely unlucky to bring the baby's cradle into the house before it was born – to do this would be tempting fate recklessly, a belief so strong that many people still hold to it today.

Only once the child had been safely delivered could the cradle enter the house. To bring good fortune on both baby and home, it was best to put the child first into a borrowed cradle, especially if it was the first-born of the family. But whether a new or old cradle was being used, it was bad luck for it to touch the ground when it was being taken to the house for the first time. And under no circumstances should it be carried empty: some food or a blanket were placed in it in some areas, but in parts of the Highlands tradition dictated that it should contain a live hen for a boy, or a live cock for a girl.

To ensure good luck

21

Rocking the baby's empty cradle after the child had been picked up was not thought wise: it would result in another baby being born into the house, and the whole round of associated customs and rituals would begin all over again.

Iron

The design of the cradle had to take into account the risk of fairy kidnap. Woods thought to have fairy-repellent properties, such as rowan and oak, were therefore especially favoured.

But even more important than the type of wood was the metal used to make the nails, and few substances were more effective than iron at warding off fairies and other ill-wishing beings.

What was considered one of the best ways of keeping the baby safe from harm sounds paradoxically dangerous to modern ears: it was thought that a newborn's best protection was to sleep with its father's dirk in the cradle. This created a powerful combi-

Dirk in the cradle

nation of charms: iron was a potent force against the fairies; the fact that the weapon belonged to the child's father was symbolic of his protection; and the handle of the knife crossed the blade at right angles, so forming the shape of a cross. Continuing the Christian theme, an open Bible could also be left either inside or by the side of the cradle.

An old tale from the west of Scotland tells the story of a young mother who, in spite of repeated warnings, one day forgot to put a Bible into her baby's cradle. She left the child on its own for a while, but when she returned the baby was crying and would not be silenced, From that day on, it cried and was never satisfied. She asked an old wise woman, who had originally come from the Highlands, to look at it, and she declared that the child was a changeling. To bring back the real child, she heated a poker in the fire till it was red hot, and approached the child, saying she was going to burn the sign of the cross on its brow. At that, the 'baby' leapt up, pushed her aside and shot up the chimney, leaving not only thick smoke and a smell of brimstone, but the real baby, safe and sound asleep in its cradle.

The Christening

The christening was a vitally important ceremony for the new baby and also for its kith and kin.

Before the Reformation, it was not always possible for the new baby to be christened quickly in rural parts of Scotland, as it could be some time before a priest might next visit the area. Under these circumstances, the parents might ask the midwife to perform a lay baptism, where three drops of water were sprinkled over the child's head to represent the Holy Trinity.

Other children might be taken to the local blacksmith for a ceremony over the anvil – again, using the protective property of iron. Although this was not considered as sacred as the real thing, it was thought to give the new baby some protection against malign forces.

The reformed Kirk, contrary to the long-established practice, decreed that the service must be held on a Sunday as soon as possible after the birth, preferably within the week, and some reports tell of babies newly born on a Saturday being carried miles to church the very next day.

Two purposes were served by a speedy christening. Firstly, it eliminated the danger of the child's being carried away by the fairies, and secondly, Christian believers could be satisfied in the knowledge that the child was a bona fide member of the church, and its soul was therefore safe. These were major considerations in times that combined the trials of a more vigorous and less compassionate religious conviction with a far higher rate of infant mortality.

To the unending torment of their parents, those unfortunate babies who died unbaptised could not be buried in sacred ground, and were deemed destined to spend eternity in a state of limbo. Without baptism, they could not enter Heaven, yet they had done nothing to warrant being sent to Hell, so they were destined to remain in this in-between state. The howling of the wind in the trees and glens of the Highlands was often attributed to the anguished cries of their spirits.

The Service

Many baptisms took place at home until the late seventeenth century, when the newly reformed Church of Scotland decreed that they should be held in a place of public worship. This was part of the Church's attempt to strengthen its influence over such key aspects of people's lives, and fines were imposed for baptisms not performed in church.

On the day of the christening, the baby was traditionally carried to the church by a young unmarried woman. She would also carry with her some food, usually cheese or bread, to give to the first man she met. If he accepted it, the baby would have good luck. Even better was if he went with the christening party at least some of the way to the church, especially if he blessed the child. If he refused the food or, even worse, turned away, the child would surely suffer misfortune. If this dire omen came to pass, any calamity that befell the child, even years later, was considered the responsibility of the person who had so blighted it.

On arrival at the church, the first step was to check if any other children were to be baptised, as the order of multiple christening ceremonies was critically important. When boys and girls were baptised on the same day, the girls should be first to the font. If a boy was first, his beard would be left behind in the water. Any girl then baptised in the same water would develop a beard in later life, while the boy would always remain smooth-faced.

When the baptismal water was poured over the baby's head, it was thought unlucky if it did not cry. This was taken as a sign that it would have a short life, and many babies must have left the service black-and-blue after being pinched by anxious mothers. But even this would not work, as the baby's crying had to be spontaneous and unforced.

Naming

The minister conducting the christening service had to be the first person to utter the new baby's name aloud. It would either be whispered to him at the crucial moment, or written down on paper and handed over. This also had the practical benefit of minimising the risk of error by any minister with less than perfect hearing.

Yet more customs had to be considered when choosing the child's name. The first child was generally named after the appropriate paternal grandparent, and the second after its mother's parents. Further children were given other family names.

The exception to this was the first son: whatever his position in the family, he was named by his father, very often after himself. This has remained a widespread custom in Scotland, although it is less common now than before. One other naming custom that seems to have died out almost completely is that of adding the suffix '-ina' to the father's name for a daughter, creating generations of Robinas, Georginas and Williaminas.

The Celebrations

The baby's christening was an occasion of great celebration for the parents and extended family. The top layer of the parents' wedding cake was – and often still is – used as the christening cake. All those present were given a 'christening piece' or 'baby's piece', which was either a portion of the cake or a piece of some specially made cheese.

After both christening and celebrations were over, the baby was not to be washed so that the power of the baptismal water would not be rinsed away. Many parents believed so strongly in the water's power that they asked for it to be bottled from the font, and took it home to avert bad luck and bring healing.

Churching

Strict rules governed the behaviour of a new mother after the birth. It was generally frowned upon for her to do anything, especially leave the house, until she had been 'churched'. This was also called 'kirking'. It did not involve any specific ceremony, but was simply the term for her first visit to church after the birth.

The period before churching was dangerous for the mother, in the same way that the days before baptism were risky for the child. Careless mothers could expect to be seized by fairies, who fiercely coveted human milk. There was no better remedy for a sickly fairy child, and the mother would be carried off and made to feed the creature until she was too weak to continue. The only way for the woman's husband to rescue her was to offer the fairies his finest mare or milking cow in exchange.

This legend is illustrated by an early nineteenth century story from the island of Arran. A young woman had just had her first child when she was spirited away by fairies. Her spirit appeared to her husband in a dream and told him that she would be passing with the fairy host on a certain night – all he had to do to save her was to throw her wedding gown over her as she went. But when the night came and he heard all the commotion of the fairies' passage, he was too afraid to go out. The next morning, his house was spattered with blood, and his wife was never seen again.

Like the christening, the churching service should therefore be held as quickly as possible, although, in contrast to modern practice, it was often two weeks after the birth before the mother got out of bed. In the Highlands, the ritual began with a procession circling the church three times in a sunwise direction.

◆ Childhood ◆ ◆

The First Birthday and Beyond

There was no shortage of advice for parents, before and after the birth. Any prospective parents would surely value the happy advice that 'Bairns are certain care but nae sure joy', while those planning a large family might be told:

> Waly, waly, bairns are bonny,
> Ane's eneuch an' twa's owre mony.

For the first year of its life, the baby's nails and hair were not cut. Hair was left to grow unchecked while nails could be bitten off but only on condition that any trimmings were very carefully disposed of: cuttings of nails and hair would be very dangerous if they fell into the hands of anyone wishing the child or its family harm. A belief in the power of such cuttings in primitive magic was a common one that seems to have been shared by many cultures worldwide. Even after the child's first birthday, the first cutting of its nails or hair should be done over an open Bible.

To weigh a baby in its first year was to tempt fate, as the child would almost certainly become weak as a result, and fail to thrive.

As the child grew, key events in its life were marked. The loss of the first tooth, for instance, had its own ritual. The tooth would be wrapped in a piece of paper or cloth, preferably together with a little salt, and hidden in a mousehole. This would bring luck and prosperity to the child as long as it remained concealed.

Fosterage

A custom which was common in a number of the Highland clans was the fostering into the chief's family of the children of lesser-born clan members. The fostered child would be nursed, educated and cared for in exactly the same way as a natural child. Such a handing over of children encouraged deep bonds of mutual loyalty in the clans.

Illegitimacy

Fosterage was also an option for wealthy families where an unmarried daughter had become pregnant. Having the baby secretly fostered allowed the family to avoid the shame and public scandal of a birth outside of marriage.

Some travellers even claimed that the illegitimate children of gentry had been handed over to them to bring up as their own.

Not all births outside marriage were regarded as shameful, although there was something of a shift in attitude after the Reformation. Sexual sins were regarded by the Church as among the most heinous, and girls who had borne illegitimate children were dressed in sackcloth and stood on the stool of repentance every Sunday as a public punishment for their shameful behaviour.

Although the strictly forbidding and often terrifying influence of the Kirk was very strong, there was also a far more relaxed and humane counter-balancing attitude to 'unlicensed' sexual behaviour in rural Scottish society – a view reflected in Robert Burns' poem, *Welcome to a Bastart Wean*:

> Welcome, my bonie, sweet, wee dochter!
> Tho' ye come her a wee unsought for,
> And tho' your comin I hae fought for
> > Baith kirk and queir;
> Yet, by my faith, ye're no unwrought for –
> > That I shall swear!

The first official statistics on illegitimate births in Scotland were published by the Registrar General in the 1850s. The figures revealed considerably higher rates than England, and much greater numbers for rural areas.

One explanation for such remarkably high illegitimacy rates could be the continued Scottish practice of irregular marriages (see p. 45). Despite the disapproval of the

Church, couples often took part in a handfasting ceremony, where they pledged to live together for a year and a day. Even if they then decided to part, any child born of such a union was the responsibility of the father, living without stigma and sharing equal rights of inheritance with any children born from subsequent marriages.

2: Marriage

It is hard to escape the conclusion that many of Scotland's centuries-old customs have gradually been discarded and forgotten in the light of scientific and medical advances of the nineteenth and twentieth centuries. But there remains one occasion in most people's lives when they will observe some type of tradition, possibly without even knowing it – at the time of their marriage. Scotland still has many customs surrounding this life-changing event.

◆ Finding a Partner ◆ ◆

In times when travel and communications were much more restricted than they are today, young people who wanted to find a partner had a much smaller pool of potential suitors on which to draw.

Predicting

Even so, those who couldn't wait to find the identity of their future spouse had various ways of predicting who they might eventually be. One popular ritual practised by men and women required three wooden bowls. One of the bowls was filled with clean water, another with dirty water and the third left empty. The would-be lover was blindfolded and led to the bowls. They would then point to one, and this gave an indication for the future. If they chose the bowl of clean water, they could look forward to a happy, honourable marriage. The bowl of dirty water meant either a dishonourable marriage, or else a union with someone who had been married before. The empty bowl meant that they would never marry. To ensure a fair result, the test was conducted on a 'best of three' basis, with the bowls moved about in between. For the result to count, the same bowl had to be chosen at least twice.

Apples

The apple is the most popular divining medium in Scottish customs for predicting a future spouse. This is probably due to its significance in the story of the Garden of Eden, where it symbolised the tree of life and knowledge.

Foretelling a spouse by using an apple

One popularly practised ritual for impatient would-be spouses instructed them to sit alone in front of a mirror at midnight with an apple cut up into pieces. All of the apple should then be eaten except the last piece, which should be thrown over their left shoulder. On turning their head to the left, an image of their future partner should appear in the mirror.

Another trick was for them to pare the skin off the apple in one piece and throw it over their left shoulder. It would land in the shape of the initial letter of their future spouse's name. But this had to be done carefully, as bad luck would result if the skin broke when it fell on the floor.

As well as some skill in peeling the apple, this custom also requires good imagination to decide what letter the skin formed. Fairly liberal interpretation combined with wishful thinking would allow almost any letter to be 'seen'!

Dreams

Dreaming of an eligible member of the opposite sex was thought to be a significant indicator that they would be a future partner. This type of premonition could even be brought on by using a piece of bride's cake (see p. 52): this was broken over the head of the new wife immediately after the wedding, and the unmarried female guests would then rush to grab a piece. For a girl to sleep with this under her pillow was an almost certain way of predicting her future partner, who would appear in her dreams that night.

Some of these customs still persist, but when they are practised today, it is done in fun rather than as a serious attempt at divination.

◆ Courting ◆ ◆

Many parts of Scotland had their own terms for courting, and one of the most common was 'winching', opportunities for which mainly centred around the local fair. These were held all over the country once or twice a year, and were an ideal opportunity for young people to get together, to see who was available and to flirt. Curious girls might also consult the fair's spaewife, who was believed to be able to foretell the future, for hints on their future spouses.

Other good occasions for meeting up with the opposite sex were the Hallowe'en celebrations, the harvest festival, or at other people's weddings. In urban areas, organised events were more common, and by the late nineteenth century, the cities' dance-halls were popular meeting places.

Bundling

Once a couple were courting, a common next step was bundling, a tradition which was practised especially in the Hebrides and other parts of the Highlands. This custom, which seemed almost to place the couple in the way of temptation, involved their going to bed together, fully clothed and possibly with a bolster between them. Sometimes the girl would be tied in a 'bundling stocking' – usually a long bolster cover secured at her waist – to prevent any hanky-panky.

Bundling was carried out with the blessing of the girl's family and was a purely practical solution to the harsh

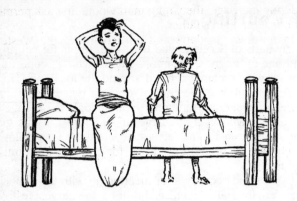

Bundling

conditions of the time and the climates in the areas where it flourished. It allowed the couple to get to known one another without interruption or interference from family members. Where large extended families lived together in two or three rooms, it was the courting couple's only chance of privacy.

Similar customs existed in other North European countries with cold climates, including Germany, Switzerland and the Scandinavian countries. Each one had its own name for the practice, and its own peculiar set of rules. It was a custom which died out fairly quickly as heating and housing conditions improved.

Rèitach

If their courtship progressed well and a couple were considering marriage, the young man would first ask permission from the girl's father.

In northern Scotland and particularly in the Western Isles, this request might take the form of a *rèitach*, a ritual which persisted into the early years of the twentieth century.

A gathering of the couple's friends would assemble on some pretext at the bride's home. One would be selected as spokesman, and he would approach her father. The conversation would apparently be about something totally different, but nevertheless analogous to the groom's situation: for example, he would say that he had heard the family had a boat or an animal that needed to be taken care of, and would volunteer to arrange it. If he was happy with the match, the father would agree to the proposal and an evening's celebration would be the inevitable result.

Considering this deliberately abstruse method of asking for permission to marry, it was obviously important that the girl's family knew the couple were thinking of marriage – the last thing the groom's spokesman wanted to get out of the evening was an unwanted pig to take care of!

◆ Betrothal ◆ ◆

Timing

When permission for the wedding was granted, the next consideration was setting the date.

The most popular month for Scottish weddings was traditionally June, a custom which continues to the present day, while May was the month with fewest marriages. 'Marry in May, rue for aye' was a common saying, based on the belief that a May wedding could only end in unhappiness, an idea which took on different forms around the country. In some places it was believed that a couple married in May would be childless, and in others that their children would not be healthy. It was also thought that the husband and wife would quickly tire of each other, or that one of them would die young.

During the last century in Glasgow, average numbers of weddings in May were around half those for the other eleven months of the year. June and July were the most popular, with numbers rising at the times of local annual holidays.

Naming the Day

The particular day of the wedding had to be chosen carefully too, as this popular rhyme demonstrates:

> Monday for wealth,
> Tuesday for health,
> Wednesday no luck at all.
> Thursday for losses,
> Friday for crosses,
> Saturday best day of all.

The rhyme took the same form across the country, but with some regional variation relating to the days. Friday was undoubtedly the most contentious, being described variously as either the best or the worst day for a wedding.

In the west of Scotland, it was thought particularly auspicious; less so in the east of the country.

Engagement

The period leading up to the day of the wedding was also marked by its own customs.

The giving of an engagement ring by a man to his fiancée is a fairly recent innovation that has become an important part of the pre-wedding celebrations for many couples. Friends of the bride may ask to try on her ring, turning it round on their finger three times and making a wish for luck.

Another custom involving the bride-to-be was the assembly of a 'bottom drawer'. Also known in Scotland as a wedding 'kist' (or chest), this would eventually contain all the table linen and bedding that she would need for her household after her marriage. The kist was sent to the couple's marital home just before the wedding, so that everything she required for her new duties would be waiting for her.

◆ Pre-Wedding Celebrations ◆ ◆

The weeks and days of anticipation before the wedding were traditionally characterised by a party atmosphere, as is still the case for many Scottish weddings.

Show of Presents

One almost exclusively female custom that has persisted is the show of presents. Now found mainly in the west of

Scotland, all the couple's wedding gifts are displayed in the bride's home. This custom was originally meant to show the bride's gratitude for the gifts, by publicly displaying them to female friends, relatives and neighbours.

The occasional male can be found at these gatherings nowadays, but on the whole a show of presents still tends to be a gathering of female family and friends of both the bride and groom. After the gifts have been duly admired, a small celebration follows. This would in the past have comprised a genteel tea with some home-baking and a bit of social chit-chat, but alcohol and dancing are now more likely to feature.

Girls' Night

The traditional 'girls' night out' for the bride has changed dramatically in recent years, mainly due to a more relaxed attitude to women drinking in pubs.

In times past, a Scots bride would be dressed up by her friends in sheets and crêpe paper. They would then present her with a chamber pot or, as these became less common with the advent of indoor toilets for all, a baby's potty full of salt; this was symbolic of her future prosperity and fertility, and she had to jump over it three times for luck. Making as much noise as possible, banging on pots and pans and shouting, her friends would then escort her through the neighbourhood streets. Any men the party came across had to kiss the bride for luck, putting a gift of coins into her pot.

Known in some areas as the bride's 'pay-off', this custom still exists in some, more rural parts of the country, especially in Ayrshire. The only real change has been the addition of alcohol, as the girls now tend to find their kiss-and cash-dispensing victims in the local pubs and clubs.

But this custom has largely been surpassed by the 'hen night', much more like a female version of a stag night, when the girls spend an evening drinking together and celebrating the forthcoming nuptials. The name comes from the ancient custom of the women involved in the wedding celebrations assembling at the home of the bride to pluck chickens for the feast.

Stag Night

This custom is not exclusively Scottish but is celebrated here as enthusiastically as anywhere, traditionally held on the groom's last night as a single man.

Changing practice in the last few years has seen the stag night shift from the night before the wedding to several days in advance. Past experience has dictated this common-sense move. It allows the prospective groom time to recover both from any over-indulgence in alcohol and from any loss of his dignity after the often elaborately organised practical jokes played on him by his friends. Victims in more extreme cases have in the past found themselves penniless on morning trains in King's Cross or Euston in London, with no idea how they got there, or stripped and left naked in a very public place.

Scotland has always had its own variation on the occasion's traditions, but these are becoming less common, replaced by strippers and kissograms (for women and men) or, for the more adventurous and less sedentary, the newly popular practice of holding stag nights in Dublin or Amsterdam.

Local variations on the humiliation theme have included, in Stonehaven, the bridegroom being 'tarred and feathered'; while in Kingussie, he was blackened with soot, boot polish or even cocoa – almost any substance that made a mess would be seized by the party! This blackening appears to be a variation of the foot-washing which is often carried out on both bride and groom together.

Feet-Washing

A symbol of the couple's fresh start in life together, the ritual feet-washing was performed on both the bride and groom, usually on the night before the wedding.

This seems to be another example of the Scandinavian influence on Scottish customs; it is very similar to the Norse tradition of the bride's bath. This was a purification ritual, performed on the bride by her unmarried friends.

Although a significant and symbolic event, this was also an excuse for horseplay, with the protesting couple's friends covering their feet and legs with soot and grease before washing it off. A ring was sometimes thrown into the water, and the person who found it would be the next of the party to marry. After the rowdy ceremonial, the rest of the night was spent singing, dancing and drinking.

◆ The Wedding ◆ ◆

Penny Weddings

Today an increased mobility for everyone ensures that

wedding guests are drawn from across the country and even further afield, but in the past weddings were very much rooted far more in the community where the couple lived.

There was very little formality attached to a traditional wedding, which was seen as a time of celebration for the whole community, with everyone in the neighbourhood welcome to join in.

This was the basis of the egalitarian and do-it-yourself celebration known as the penny wedding. Every guest would contribute money which was put towards the cost of the food, drink and music. Any extra that was left over would be given to the newly married couple to help start their new life together.

Penny weddings were characterised by much revelry, dancing and drunkenness and, not surprisingly, were much frowned-upon by the religious authorities. The national moral guardians in the Church of Scotland spoke out against them several times in the seventeenth and eighteenth centuries, colourfully calling them 'seminaries of all profanation'. Fines of £2 Scots were imposed on members of the congregation who took part, but even this had very little effect.

Many Scottish weddings are still conducted along very much the same lines; unlike English celebrations, the party continues well into the night, although this tradition recently seems to be spreading south of the border. Given the great expense involved in organising such an event, it is now the custom for family and close friends to attend the service and meal afterwards, with other guests invited along for the evening celebration.

Bad Omens

Every aspect of the wedding day attracted its own particular custom and superstition. Any unexpected event, no
matter how apparently trivial, was thought to be ominous.
Recorded examples of such seemingly innocuous happen-
ings include a dog howling nearby; the (probably nervous)
bride accidentally breaking a dish; and soot falling out of
the chimney – all of these were considered to be ill omens.

Seeing a funeral procession on the way to or from the
wedding was a particularly serious and dire omen. This
was a sign that one of the pair would die young. If the
deceased was female, the bride would soon die; if male,
the groom would not last long past the wedding day.

Another sure sign of an ill-starred match was if the bride
looked back on leaving her home to go to the wedding.
This meant that she would not be happy in her new home.

To bring the bride good luck on her wedding day, and to
allow all who saw her to wish her well, her carriage – or
today her wedding car – should be decked out in white
ribbons.

The Wedding Dress

Formal wedding wear did not catch on in Scotland until
the twentieth century. Instead it was traditional for the
bride to have a new dress made for the occasion, although
it was bad luck for her to make it all herself.

The now-traditional white dress was introduced by
Queen Victoria, in a custom much copied and not just in
Scotland. Previously almost any colour was acceptable
except the mourning colours, black and navy. Green was

also avoided: as the colour traditionally associated with fairies (see p. 161), it could attract their unwanted attention.

One lasting tradition is adhered to, with the bride wearing 'something old, something new, something borrowed, something blue'. The last part of this custom, 'and a silver sixpence in her shoe', can also still be found, with the bride putting a silver coin in her shoe to represent the couple's future prosperity in their life together.

Whatever their outfits, when the bride and groom were dressed they would untie all the knots on their clothing before the ceremony. This would remove any barriers to their fertility once they were married.

The Wedding Ring

The wedding ring, symbol of the pledge made by the bride and groom, dates back to Roman times. The custom of placing the ring on the third finger of the bride's left hand was banned after the Reformation of 1560, as it was considered to be a popish tradition, but was eventually restored in the second half of the seventeenth century.

Recently, more and more men have taken to wearing a wedding ring, although some Scotsmen are still resistant to the idea. However, the practice has become so widespread nowadays that the marriage service has been adapted to include an exchange of rings between bride and groom.

Irregular Marriage

Today's strictly regulated marriage laws, with their terms

and conditions, deadlines and restrictions, make it hard to imagine the relatively relaxed attitude to marriage which existed in Scotland in the past. But until legal changes were made in the twentieth century, there was no need for a celebrant, witnesses or even cohabitation to make a marriage legal in Scotland. The only necessary criterion was consent. Both parties should be free to marry, and should make a declaration of their intention to live as husband and wife. The Kirk, perceiving a threat to challenge its total grip on Scottish society, insisted in vain from the time of its establishment after the Reformation that marriage should be performed in a place of worship.

Marriage by 'custom and repute' was also widely accepted. If a couple had lived together for a number of years as husband and wife, they were considered to be married, and had many of the same rights as formally married couples.

Handfasting

This intriguing practice was followed in many areas of Scotland. The name handfasting – itself thought to be a form of trial marriage – translates as 'pledging the hand', and similar terms were used in Anglo-Saxon and some Scandinavian languages.

The ceremony was often performed at the annual fair, and involved the couple pledging to live together for a year and a day. When this time was up, they could choose to marry at the next fair in the following year. If they chose to part at the end of the allocated time, no stigma was attached to either of them, and even if their temporary union produced children, they were not considered illegitimate. It was the responsibility of their father to look after the children, and they enjoyed exactly the same rights as the offspring of any more formal, religious marriage.

Although the idea may be Norse in origin, the legal aspects of handfasting may have their origins in a Roman law, which decreed that if a man and woman lived together for a year without being apart for three nights, they were considered to be married. Another, more Scottish source for the practice may have been the Celtic tradition of clasping hands through a special stone to seal a contract. These were known as swearing stones, and one example is Odin's Stone on Orkney.

Handfasting and other types of irregular marriage were only outlawed as recently as 1939.

The modern idea of a couple living together before marriage or, as it is sometimes called, having a 'trial marriage', has been much frowned upon in many Scottish communities, especially among older people. This disapproval has even extended to the places where handfasting was practised in the past. It may be explained by the

Clasping hands at a swearing stone

Church's attitude to such matters after the Reformation, when fornication and adultery came to be treated as shameful sins, to be punished with public penance.

Church Weddings

As the influence of the Church in marriage gradually took hold, religious ceremonies became increasingly common and are still the preferred option for most Scottish couples.

Before the service could take place, the banns of marriage had to be proclaimed on three consecutive Sundays in the church where the wedding was due to take place. This announced to the neighbourhood the couple's intention to marry, and alerted anyone who might have any reason to object.

On the day of the wedding, those attending the service usually walked to the church in two parties of the bride and groom with their respective friends, headed by their fathers. If the journeys had been planned properly, the two groups should arrive simultaneously. In the Highlands, before a bridal party entered the church for the service it was customary for them to circle the church building three times in a sunwise direction.

If more than one couple was to be married at the same time, the first pair out of the church were believed to have the most promising start to their life together. This accounts for a number of sprints for the door reported at the end of a number of joint weddings.

It was thought lucky to be first to kiss the bride after the service and, because of his central role in the proceedings, this was an honour that customarily fell to the minister.

Good fortune could be brought to the newlyweds by making plenty of noise. How this was done depended on the time – in the past by ringing the church bells or cheering, and nowadays by honking car horns and other kinds of din – all have been common. This was in part celebratory, to let the neighbourhood know of the happy event, but its origins lie in the tradition of creating a loud noise to frighten off any evil spirits who could bring ill luck to the marriage.

After the wedding, the guests formed one party, led by the fathers of the bride and groom, then the newly-weds. The group would proceed to the couple's new home for the customary celebrations.

Waiting for the scatter

◆ Post-Wedding Celebrations ◆ ◆

The Scatter

As the couple left the church after their wedding, the guests would throw a shower of rice or confetti over them as a symbol of fertility. The groom would then throw a handful of coins to local children who would gather at the church door for the 'scramble' or 'scatter', as it was known in various areas.

The small bands of hopeful and determined-looking children who still gather at church gates for wedding ceremonies are testimony to the custom's enduring popularity.

Running the Broose

When the marriage service was over, the younger male guests would join in the custom of running the broose or braise. This was a race back to the groom's home, and the first one back would win a bottle of whisky which was drunk to toast the newly wedded couple's health.

This light-hearted tradition probably had a darker past, in the Scandinavian practice of wife-stealing, where a man would kidnap a woman he wanted to marry and force her to go through with the ceremony. His family would wait at home in case a rescue bid was mounted by the woman's family, and when the service was over the groom's supporters would rush back, either on foot or on horseback, to let them know that everything was completed safely (for the man, at least). The traditional prize for the bearer of these happy tidings was a bowl of brose.

Dancing

A lavish meal would be held after the wedding to celebrate the happy event, culminating in drinking and dancing among the guests. In recent years, a definite order has
become established for dancing. First on the floor for the
opening dance are the new husband and wife, followed by
the best man and bridesmaid, then both sets of parents.
The dances included reels, strathspeys and hornpipes,
such as the popular *Dashing White Sergeant* and the exuberant and energetic *Strip the Willow*. In the past, any still-
unmarried older sister of the bride's had to parade her
man-less failure publicly, as she was made to dance bare-
foot. The dancing would be brought to an end by the
assembled guests singing *Auld Lang Syne*, linking hands to
form a circle around the couple.

Bride's Cake

Different from the modern wedding cake was the Bride's Cake of bannock or shortbread, the traditional wedding cake of Scotland. The bride's mother would crumble it over her daughter's head, confetti-like, as she entered her new home after the wedding. If the cake broke into lots of small pieces, the marriage was destined to be fruitful; if it did not, this was taken as a sign of possible infertility. The remains of the cake were then fought over by the young unmarried women guests to help them dream of their future husband (see p. 34).

After the crumbling of the cake, the bride's new mother-in-law would give her the keys of the house, transferring responsibility for taking care of the groom from his mother to his wife. The bride was also given the fire tongs and poker, symbolic or her new responsibility for the home.

When the celebrations were drawing to a close for the evening, the bride's friends would prepare her for bed. The groom's friends then sent him into the bedchamber,

The bride's mother would crumble the cake over her head

52

and the rest of the wedding party followed. One of the bride's stockings was thrown to the assembled guests – this was a sought-after prize, as the person who caught it would be the next one to be married. A similar custom exists today, but the stocking has been replaced by the bride's bouquet. The assembled guests raised their glasses to the happy couple for the last time, before leaving.

Wedding Cake

The wedding cake has become a central part of the celebrations of modern weddings, not just in Scotland but in most other western countries.

The first records of wedding cake being eaten at a Scots wedding date from the seventeenth century, and an eighteenth century recipe from Edinburgh for a Bride's Pie includes what seems to modern eyes an odd mixture of calf's feet, beef suet, apples, raisins, cinnamon, lemon peel, brandy and champagne. This Christmas Pudding-like confection developed gradually into the heavy fruit cake customarily eaten at weddings today. Increasingly in recent years, however, more couples have been departing from the customary fruit cake and choosing other types of cake, according to their preference.

Cutting the cake is a symbolic act performed by the bride, who is helped by her new husband. The cake's top layer should be kept for use as a christening cake for the couple's first child. All the wedding guests are given a portion, and any left over is returned to the bride and groom, to be cut up and sent out to friends not at the wedding – either those who were invited but could not come, or those who gave the couple gifts but were not invited.

◆ After The Wedding ◆ ◆

Coming Home

One very well-known wedding tradition that is still wide-ly practiced, and not just in Scotland, is the convention of the bride being carried over the threshold by her husband. This is to ensure that she does not trip or fall on her first step into her new home, as this would be a sign of sure misfortune in the future.

Family and friends would pass on their best wishes to the couple in their home, many using the traditional Scottish blessing for the home, 'Lang may yer lum reek. This goodwill wish literally means, 'Long may your chimney smoke', hoping for a long, happy and prosperous life in the new home.

The curtch

Churching

As the newly weds adjust-ed to their life together, there was one last symbol-ic ceremony to perform. On the first Sunday after the wedding, the couple would attend church together, dressed up to the nines, and accompanied by their best man and bridesmaid. This first official outing after the marriage was known as the kirking (or churching) of the bride. It was regarded as the final confirmation of their married status, and from that point on they were seen as husband and wife rather than bride and groom.

In the past, a married woman would customarily wear a curtch, a type of linen cap to cover her hair, as an outward sign that she was married. It was often a square of linen, folded in half diagonally, and wrapped around the head close to the hairline. The ends would then be fastened at the nape of the neck, although some older women preferred to tie it under the chin. A bride would usually be given one of these caps as a gift from her married friends, to signify her new status as a married woman, and as a sign that she had left behind her girlhood, as represented by loose and uncovered hair.

The woman was then expected to start the traditional and undoubtedly the most morbid duty of every new wife. She should begin spinning a winding-sheet, or shroud, for herself and

Creeling

one for her new husband. The completed items, known as their 'deid claes', would be kept in storage for as long as necessary, brought out to be washed and aired occasionally, and jealously guarded.

Creeling

The new husband also had to face his own friends for their particular post-wedding rituals, of which 'creeling' was a common one in many areas across the country.

The groom's friends would attach a creel, or basket, to his back. Leaving him in no doubt as to what he had taken on, they would fill it with large stones, representing his new responsibilities.

◆ Elopement ◆ ◆

Gretna Green

Not every traditional wedding in Scotland followed these customary patterns. Over the years an alternative tradition developed, although its participants often came from outside the country. This was the practice of quick marriages, usually as a result of elopement, by young people from England.

The age of consent for marriage in Scotland has for centuries been sixteen. In England, twenty-one was the age of maturity, although this later changed to eighteen. There was therefore a great temptation for young and impetuous couples who had decided to marry against their parents' wishes to do so in Scotland. All that was required for such a union was two consenting participants over the age of sixteen who were free to marry.

Although couples from outside Scotland could be married anywhere in the country, they tended to stop at the first possible point across the border. Coldstream Bridge and Lamberton Toll were popular spots, but it was neighbouring Gretna Green, further to the west and on a main highway, that quickly became synonymous with such weddings. It was the most accessible Borders town on the road from London to Scotland via Carlisle.

When the similarly quick and easy 'Fleet' marriages were outlawed in England in 1754, weddings in Scotland became even more popular with couples from south of the border.

In the first half of the nineteenth century, records show between 50 and 200 marriages a year for just one of the many 'marrying-men' in the Borders area. One of the most famous of these was Joseph Paisley, a Borders man whose previous career had been unsettled, to say the least, before he discovered the lucrative marriage trade. He worked with David Long, his nephew, and this family practice was eventually joined by Robert Elliot, who married Paisley's granddaughter – in the village church! Although all of these men had worked at a variety of jobs, including fishing and trading, there is no mention of any of them being employed as a blacksmith – the trade traditionally thought of as that of the marrying man.

Over the Anvil

The popular idea of couples eloping to be married by a blacksmith is not strictly accurate. The celebrants came

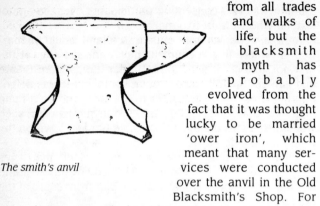

from all trades and walks of life, but the blacksmith myth has p r o b a b l y evolved from the fact that it was thought lucky to be married 'ower iron', which meant that many services were conducted over the anvil in the Old Blacksmith's Shop. For around 300 years, 'Blacksmith's marriage' was a common term for all irregular marriages.

The smith's anvil

Elopement Scandals

Not surprisingly, elopements and hastily arranged weddings scandalised nineteenth-century sensibilities, although some classic cases gained particular notoriety. The most infamous Gretna Green elopement was the 1826 case of Ellen Turner, the fifteen-year-old daughter of a wealthy mill owner, and trickster Edward Gibbon Wakefield. Wakefield falsely told the girl a story that her father had given permission for them to marry because the Turner family business had suddenly run into trouble, and Wakefield had money that could save it. It says much for the lack of communication between Ellen and her father that she agreed to the marriage without further reference to him, and the pair were soon married at Gretna Green.

Her father had not given his permission, of course, and launched a search for the couple. When they were tracked down, Wakefield was prosecuted in what became a sensational and highly scandalous case. The legality of the marriage was questioned as Ellen was under sixteen, and the marriage was declared void. Wakefield was sentenced to three years in Newgate Gaol.

Legislation

As the railway reached Carlisle and access to Gretna weddings became even easier, pressure grew for the government to curb these speedy services. In 1856, Lord Brougham's Act was passed by parliament, stipulating that either the bride or groom had to be resident in Scotland for at least three weeks before the wedding.

Considering the purely commercial nature of the Gretna marriage services, it is difficult to asses how effective this legislation would have been. While it may have slowed the flood of eloping couples, it is more than possible that the celebrants could have been persuaded to overlook something potentially so difficult to prove as the residency clause.

The 1939 Marriage (Scotland) Act ended the legality of Gretna Green weddings, but couples from all over the world still make the journey to the small Borders town to make their marriage vows. Now the legal ceremony is conducted, as elsewhere, by a registrar or cleric, and the couples involved have rarely eloped. The main industry at Gretna Green these days is probably tourism, but this is one old Scottish wedding tradition that continues, at least in some form.

◆ Continuing Traditions ◆ ◆

Inevitably, many of Scotland's old wedding customs have either been forgotten or allowed to die out, eroding a particular part of the country's distinctive heritage. But as these past traditions die, new ones constantly evolve out of them to take their place. There may be no more *rèitachs* or bundling, but social and cultural changes across the country will still bring about the development of new traditions. However, as in other spheres of life, these newcomers will very probably lack the distinctively Scottish approach that their predecessors possessed.

3: *Death*

As with birth, so the common attitude to death in Scotland has undergone a dramatic change, particularly in the light of modern medical advances, improved living conditions and the general decline in religious belief.

The Scottish attitude to death was for centuries one of a philosophical resignation in the face of the inevitable. There was a common acceptance that the only sure thing in life was death – a fatalistic attitude amply illustrated in the stereotypically morose and joy-puncturing Scots proverb, 'Oor first breath is the beginning o' daith'. In more recent times, though, death has become less of a preoccupation for Scots than it was in times past. Most people have little direct contact with mortality, even among their own family, as so many people die in hospitals, hospices and nursing homes, with their bodies being swiftly transported to funeral parlours and thence to crematoriums or burial grounds.

◆ Signs and Portents ◆ ◆

Signs and events which were interpreted as omens of death were common all over the country, some of them confined to a particular area, and others accepted nationally.

One myth that seems to have been fairly widespread was the 'deid-drap'. This regular noise, like dripping water or a ticking sound , was heard in the house, usually in an empty room or in the room of an invalid, and did not bode well for the recovery of any sick person. In reality, the noise was probably made by woodworm or other insects inside the fabric of the house or the furniture. But in the quiet of a sickroom, these sounds would be more audible than normal and they were interpreted as a sign of the patient's approaching death.

A vision of a person who was ill was another indication of their imminent passing. If someone saw a person who was known to be ill, on the street for example, and after passing by, looked back at them only to see no-one there, the spectre was an omen of death. This was believed to be especially true if the sighting was in the evening or at night.

Another sinister sign was a ringing in the ears. Anyone who had this extremely common sensation would shortly hear news of a death.

Dead candles or lights were often seen around the home or garden of someone who was about to die. These were bluish lights, like will-o'-the-wisp, that hovered just above the ground.

Animal Behaviour

Dogs were considered to be particularly sensitive to an impending death. A dog barking or howling in the night was a sure sign of someone's end approaching. In the north-east, this omen was interpreted more specifically – the dog was thought to face in the direction of the victim.

The behaviour of birds was also closely observed and interpreted. A hen that crowed like a cock, a cock crowing during the night, or a bird tapping on the window were ominous signs, especially if there was an ill person in the house. A raven or a heron could also be a harbinger of death.

Swallows were also considered significant. To destroy a swallow's nest meant bringing death on the family within 18 months; to have the bird nesting in the house was a sign of luck and prosperity, and to tempt fate by tearing it down was verging on the suicidal.

Interpretation

Many Scots believed that these warnings were given to those about to die so they could prepare themselves and make their peace with God.

However, they may also have been self-fulfilling prophesies at times. There were doubtless occasions when a sick person who would otherwise have made a full recovery actually died, their will to recover sapped by some traditional omen that convinced them their end had come, and taking too much to heart the words of the traditional proverb: 'Daith is deaf and will hear nae denial'.

On the other hand, there must also have been times when, despite the omens and signs, the invalid recovered. On these occasions, the doom-laden prophesies would be conveniently forgotten or subsequently re-interpreted in a different way.

Superstitions

It was not just omens and portents of death that Scots have had to look out for over the centuries. It was also believed that impending doom lurked behind many apparently innocent actions.

Putting shoes on a table is still looked on with dread by many people, as is a vase containing red and white flowers together.

Another way to tempt fate would be to take a broom or a spade into the house – an act which would almost certainly be followed by the death of someone in the family.

◆ After Death ◆ ◆

Passage of the Soul

Even after the Reformation, it was still possible to find in Scotland evidence of the traditional Celtic belief that the soul needed a passage physically cleared to allow it to make its way to God. To this end, seriously ill people would be lifted up out of bed and laid down on the floor to facilitate their soul's journey – not particularly reassuring for the invalid involved. Another way of easing the soul's way was to open all the locks and doors in the house, so that there were no barriers or hindrances to its passage.

Protecting the Departing Soul

To protect the soul from any evil forces, all the curtains and blinds in the house would be closed. Clocks in the room were stopped at the moment of death, and mirrors and pictures were covered or turned to face the wall, so that the soul would not be confused and become trapped behind the glass.

All animals and pets were kept out of the room where the corpse lay. A cat or a dog jumping over the body could affect the soul's progress and result in its being taken over by the Devil. Any unfortunate animal that did stray into the sickroom might be killed immediately to stop it from affecting the passage to the afterlife.

Spreading the News

A significant part of the Scottish ritual following a death was the ringing of the 'dead-bell'. This hand-held bell often hung from a tree or the gate of the graveyard, and was rung by either a friend of the family, or whoever usually rang the church bells. This instant way of spreading news was especially important in times before newspapers as a quick way of notifying friends and neighbours of the death. The bell's clanging also had a spiritual side, as its noise was thought to frighten away any evil spirits trying to capture the soul. It may also have been a hang-over from the medieval practice of ringing the church bells after a death to remind people to pray for the souls of the departed.

In the nineteenth and early twentieth century on Lewis, young boys were given sixpence to run around informing the local people after a death, and giving them details of the funeral arrangements.

Nowadays, death notices in newspapers are a widely

accepted method of notifying anyone concerned of a death. It is also fairly common for these to be followed on the anniversary of the death by an 'In Memoriam' notice, remembering the life of the individual and often accompanied by a standard verse.

Tending the Body

After a death a whole array of customs relating to the corpse had to be observed. Its eyes had to be closed, for fear that the deceased might see someone else to take with them. Coins would sometimes be placed on the eyelids, in a custom common to many other countries, to make sure that the eyes remained closed. This could also have been an echo of the ancient pre-Christian belief in taking material possessions into the afterlife.

A dish of salt would be placed on the corpse's chest, as this was sup-posed to pre-vent the body from swelling after death. Salt is a feature of many Scottish traditions as a symbol of good fortune, and it may have ful-filled a similar

Coins were placed on the eyes of the dead

purpose here, preventing malevolent forces from disturbing the body.

The body would be washed and dressed in a simple winding sheet. In the days before commercial undertakers this was hand-made, and the sewing of burial shrouds for herself and her husband was one of the happy first tasks which awaited any new bride in Scotland until at least the nineteenth century. Even if they had been in storage for sixty or seventy years, the 'deid claes' should be in immaculate condition, as they were lovingly aired and looked after.

Sin-Eaters

A remarkable phenomenon found in some other countries, but also reported in pre-Reformation Scotland, was the 'sin-eater'. This was a person hired before the funeral to sit with the corpse and eat some symbolic food – usually bread – to represent the sins of the deceased. This would allow the soul to journey straight to heaven, without first having to do penance in Purgatory for the sins the person had committed in their lifetime.

The Sin-Eater

◆ The Funeral ◆ ◆

The Wake

The wake took place on the night before the funeral and was an occasion to celebrate the deceased's life and the passage of their soul on to a better place.The participants were a few of the dead person's family and close friends, who would sit up with the corpse the whole night, not leaving it alone for a minute. At this time the soul was particularly susceptible to the influence of the evil eye, and lit candles would be placed all round the body to protect it.

The vigilance of those present did not forbid them from seeking sustenance and as much enjoyment as such a grim situation allowed, and a wake was usually marked by drinking whisky and telling stories through the night. The very nature of the situation often led the minds of those present towards ghost stories, which would have made for some spine-tingling times! At Highland wakes, bagpipes or fiddles were brought along, and laments played.

Of course, things often got out of hand. An account of a Highland funeral tells of a funeral party, still drunk from the wake the night before, journeying miles through the snow to the burial ground, only to find there was no body for them to bury – the corpse had inconveniently slid off its cart some miles back and had gone unnoticed in the melée.

The traditional Scottish wake appears to have known no class barriers. An account of the expenses for the wake of Sir David Campbell of Ardnamurchan, who died in 1651, shows a total bill for food and drink of over £189 Scots, £84 of which was for the whisky alone.

The Wake

After the Reformation, this kind of stoical jollity in the face of death was frowned upon, and in 1645 the Kirk's General Assembly, its governing body, spoke out against the traditional wake. But its disapproval must have fallen on deaf ears, as the same body issued the same type of edict again a few decades later. It is fair to assume that the ban was again disregarded, as these all-night wakes can still be found in parts of Scotland. Now, however, the wake is usually performed out of habit and a mark of respect for the dead. Recent times have seen the original motive – that an unattended body could be carried off by the Devil or his minions – forgotten or at least dismissed as an ancient superstition.

Undertakers

Undertakers did not really come into being until the early nineteenth century, when some wealthy Scots families began to use the services of these specialists in death rituals. This was the real beginning of the process of distancing ourselves from death that is now considered normal.

The first undertakers in Glasgow emerged in 1832, during the city's devastating cholera epidemic of that time. The authorities could find no-one to dispose of the bodies of the victims, until two enterprising young carpenters called Wylie and Lochhead offered their services. Their offer was accepted and their business flourished to such an extent that it still buries Glaswegians today, over 150 years later.

Until the 1950s, it was usual for the body to stay in the house for at least three days after death. This would allow plenty of time for the necessary customs to be followed, and for family and friends to pay their last respects. In Catholic families, the body is usually taken to the church the night before the funeral. A Mass is said that evening, and the body is left overnight in the church, surrounded by candles.

Funeral Preparations

Before the advent of undertakers, the corpse would be prepared for burial by close female family and friends. It would be washed, anointed and laid out in the winding sheet before the 'kistan' – the ceremonial placing of the body in its coffin. This could be a fairly brutal affair. If the body had been left contorted for any reason after the onset of rigor mortis, the limbs would be unceremoniously broken and rearranged to make the corpse lie flat in the coffin.

Last Respects

The lid would be left off the coffin until the last possible moment before the funeral, to allow anyone who wished to see and touch the body. Touching the corpse was considered particularly important, not just in terms of paying their last respects, but to prevent anyone who looked on the deceased being haunted by their ghost.

Anyone who did not take part in this traditional practice, including women and children, could expect to be plagued with nightmares for weeks and months to come.

This custom of touching the corpse could also prove useful in any case where murder was suspected. If the dead body was touched by its murderer, it would begin to bleed, thereby providing a sign for the other mourners of exactly who the guilty party was.

Coffins

The Victorian era saw the development of increasingly elaborate death customs all over the country. These were slow to catch on in many parts of Scotland, particularly the Highlands, but they still influence the way death is dealt with today.

Until undertakers took over the task of coffin construction in the nineteenth century, coffins were simple wooden boxes, often of oak, usually knocked together by a local joiner or carpenter. But they, and their accessories, became more elaborate with the advent of professional funeral services. Instead of a plain coffin and shroud, the dead came to be buried in ornate and expensive coffins, lined with velvet or satin and decorated with extravagant handles and fittings. Families who could afford it also began dressing the corpse in fine clothes.

For those who could not afford the trappings of an expensive funeral, a re-usable pauper's coffin was developed in the eighteenth century. The bottom of the coffin slid back, allowing the corpse to be deposited in the grave without the coffin, which was taken away to be used again.

The Funeral Ceremony

But it was not just the corpse who was dressed in special clothes. In pre-Victorian times, mourners would dress in their best clothes for a funeral, showing their respect, although few would have bought a special outfit just for this service.

Following the example set by Queen Victoria in her mourning of Prince Albert, black has been accepted as the customary colour for funeral clothes. Victoria wore black from the time of Albert's death in 1861 until her own, four decades later. In fact, her mourning was so long that a whole new fashion offshoot grew up around it, with jet mourning jewellery and other accessories which have, in the less formal intervening century, long fallen into disuse.

Even in the first half of the twentieth century, women were expected to dress entirely in black for a year after the death of their husband. After this initial period of public mourning, they could introduce grey or pale purples into their wardrobes for a further six months. The code for men was slightly less restrictive: they were expected to wear a black armband for some time after their wife's burial, and even today a black tie for funerals is a standard in the wardrobes of most Scottish men.

Mourners began to send sympathy cards in Victorian times, with Catholics sending Mass cards, promising a Mass to be said to pray for the peaceful repose of the soul of the deceased. All these cards are still commonly sent to bereaved relatives after a death.

Funeral Processions

In the Highlands, walking funerals were customary in the past. The coffin was not placed on a cart, but was carried all the way to the burial ground by the mourners on two long spokes or poles. The closest male family members were the usual carriers, but it was not unheard of for women to bear the coffin at least part of the way. In many areas of the Highlands, especially the north east, female family and friends would carry the coffin for the first part of the journey.

The progress of such a funeral party was obviously very reliant on the weather, and the journey of the soul was believed to parallel the walk to the graveyard. Fine weather or a slight shower was felt to signify an easy passage for the soul, but a storm was considered a particularly bad sign.

A custom observed in the Borders stated that any man meeting a funeral procession should remove his hat, then turn and accompany the procession a short distance. To neglect this custom would bring serious misfortune on him, and his own death would shortly follow.

As cars became more common in the twentieth century they also have acquired a part of the funeral procession. The coffin is taken to and from the ceremony in a black hearse, with close family following in specially hired cars. Mourners then follow behind in a procession of their cars.

Burial or Cremation?

This question has only been raised in Scotland since the 1950s. Before this, burial was traditionally the accepted custom all over Scotland.

Cremation is now the preferred option for many people, particularly in a secular funeral. Such services are becoming more common in Scotland, particularly in larger towns and cities, and are developing their own distinctive rituals. They are usually requested by people who have no particular religious beliefs and who feel that a church funeral would be hypocritical. At present, they often consist of a very simple ceremony at a crematorium, including a eulogy by a close friend or family member.

Graveyards

'A blind man will find his way to the burial ground' – a translation of an old Gaelic proverb illustrating the traditional recognition of death as the great leveller. But this belief was challenged by developments in the nineteenth century, when the middle and upper classes began to adopt new burial customs, usually involving displays of the wealth that the deceased had accrued in life.

The Glasgow Necropolis

Examples of the new nineteenth-century approach to death can be seen in the fabulously ornate Glasgow Necropolis, opened in 1832, and its sister cemetery the Southern Necropolis, which opened nine years later. These vast and spooky graveyards became home to row upon row of ostentatious and elaborate mausoleums and vaults, specially built by the wealthy families of the city to serve as displays both of their grieving and of their ability to pay.

Position

The actual situation of the burial plot was another factor to be taken into consideration. The preferred site was on the south side of the churchyard, which was felt to be closer to God's right hand. Evidence of this is seen in older churchyards, where the graves to the north of the church are usually much more recent than those to the south.

In the Highlands, it was believed that the last person buried in a graveyard had to keep watch in case a suicide or an unbaptised child was buried there. This duty was then taken over by the next deceased. When they were buried in unconsecrated ground, the bodies of suicides and the unbaptised were usually buried close to a wall or in some other position that would stop anyone from stepping over them. This was most unlucky and in the case of a pregnant woman, it was believed to bring on miscarriage.

◆ After the Funeral ◆ ◆

The Meal

A Scottish burial tradition of long standing which is still observed today is the custom of mourners, particularly close family and friends, attending a meal together. Attendance was a mark of respect for the dead and a gesture of support for the grieving family.

For families who were left short of money, sometimes the mourners at the funeral would donate some money to cover the funeral expenses. As was the case with the

Penny Wedding (see p. 42), when all the costs of the food and drink had been met, any remaining cash would go to the widow or widower and family.

After the meal for the family and friends, the 'deid dole' used to be handed out. This was based on the pre-Reformation custom of giving alms to the poor to pray for the souls of the dead, and beggars, known as 'guisers', would gather after a funeral for food or money until the early nineteenth century when the tradition seems to have stopped.

The Role of Women

The part played by Scotland's women in the various rituals surrounding death has undergone dramatic change in the second half of the twentieth century.

Until the 1950s, it was extremely rare for a woman to go with the funeral party to the graveyard. Instead, they would stay at the deceased's home, comforting the female members of the family, and preparing the food for the meal after the funeral. While older women may still prefer not to go to a graveyard, this is a custom which has largely now withered. The post-funeral meal is still found after most Scottish funerals, although a pub or hotel, with the catering laid on, is the preferred venue over the home.

Women, now leading more multi-stranded and complicated lives, no longer choose the simple role of caring for the home and family alone and this is a change increasingly reflected in the country's customs.

Yet in general, modern funerals in Scotland still follow the same basic format that they have done for centuries. The funeral service is followed by a committal, ending with a gathering of family and friends for refreshments. Some of the surrounding customs may become obsolete, or their roots forgotten, but there is no reason to believe that this will change substantially in the future.

◆ The Resurrection Men ◆ ◆

Many of the customs observed at the time of a death in Scotland are based on rituals to protect the corpse against the Devil and other evil spirits. But in the early nineteenth century, bereaved families in parts of the country had more than supernatural threats to contend with, as the activities of the resurrectionists, or body snatchers, came to the attention of a horrified public.

The new science of anatomy was advancing, particularly in Edinburgh, but its students required access to bodies. The legitimate supplies from executed criminals and paupers were not enough, and some entrepreneurs of the time decided to find their own. A lucrative trade in corpses began in the 1820s.

Precautions

There was great public revulsion at the very idea of their loved ones' bodies being desecrated in such a way, and precautions were taken in many graveyards to guard against body snatching. Watchhouses were built in many cemeteries, where a watchman would keep a look out over the graves. The watchhouse was a small stone structure, built at a position of the graveyard that left as much as possible visible. There were narrow slits in the walls for looking through or, on occasion, shooting out of. They were manned either by local men who wanted to watch over the remains of their loved ones or by professional watchmen. The latter quickly developed a bad reputation for drunkenness and laziness, with some graves robbed right under their noses. Given their extremely spooky surroundings, the watchmen were often very jumpy. One in Aberdeen shot and killed a pig that had strayed into the cemetery, and there were no doubt other incidents.

Mortsafes were also developed, heavy iron cages that were placed over the graves to protect them and embedded in the soil. They could be hoisted up and moved to another part of the graveyard if they were needed for another member of the family.

A group of Quakers in the east had a portable mortsafe designed. This was a stout iron cage that was secured around the coffin, serving the same purpose as the larger ones. When the body had deteriorated to the point where it was no longer of use, the mortsafe was dug up and kept until the next death.

Burke and Hare

The resurrectionists' activities had caused an outcry in Edinburgh and other affected areas, but they paled in comparison with the crimes of the infamous Burke and Hare.

Although both William Burke and William Hare came originally from Ireland, their place in Scottish history and folklore is guaranteed. After meeting the renowned and respected Edinburgh anatomist Dr Robert Knox, the pair became briefly involved in the resurrectionist business.

But Knox's constant need for fresh bodies and apparent lack of concern over how they were acquired, coupled with their own greed, took the trade a step further and saw them embark on a series of murders.

Burke and Hare chose their victims from the edges of society – tramps, prostitutes and beggars who would not be easily missed. Each victim was lured to the pair's flat with promises of alcohol. Once they were drunk, Burke and Hare suffocated them and sold the body on to Dr Knox. Over the course of 1828, they disposed of sixteen people in this way.

As they literally got away with murder, Burke and Hare became increasingly careless and were caught at the end of 1828 when a visitor to the flat discovered one of their victims. Hare, by all accounts the more villainous of the two, turned king's evidence against his accomplice, and Burke was hanged the next year. Hare himself was forced to leave Scotland, and Dr Knox, although cleared of any personal involvement, saw his brilliant career stopped in its tracks and his reputation ruined by this most notorious of Scottish scandals.

4: *Festivals*

*T*raditional celebrations and festivals are still very much taken for granted as an everyday part of life all over Scotland. These festivals, national and local, go on all year round and are enjoyed by all walks of life and all sectors of society.

From the ancient fire processions dating back to the time of the Druids to urban celebrations of the arts, far more recent in origin, traditional festivities still retain a strong hold over people's imagination and everyday life in Scotland.

◆ Winter ◆ ◆

Christmas

Ancient Yule celebrations by the pagan Celts took place around the time of the winter solstice, a traditional time of celebration to brighten the year's darkest days. Like other Druidic beliefs, its significance centred around the worship of the sun, and its purpose was to persuade the sun to return. The Christian Church gradually took over the festival for one of its own major celebrations, and the date of Christmas was confirmed as 25 December by the Romans.

Yet some Christmas traditions still followed today continue to betray the festival's pagan roots. The Yule log, which is burned in some fireplaces over the Christmas period, is symbolic of the communal Yule bonfire; kissing under the mistletoe may be related to a Druidic fertility rite (mistletoe was a plant revered by the Druids); and decorating the house with holly is a reminder of the reverence with which evergreen trees were regarded in winter, as a sign of life at a time of barrenness.

But there was a disruption to Scotland's traditional celebrations of Christmas after the Reformation of 1560, as the new Church of Scotland, the Kirk, frowned on what it regarded as a popish festival. In 1575, the Aberdeen Kirk Session brought charges and disciplinary proceedings against people who had been caught keeping Yule. Similar cases were reported in Glasgow in 1583. Astonishingly, this dour, joy-crushing attitude maintained its grip on the country for four centuries and until the 1960s, Christmas Day was a normal working day for many Scots as their winter festivities centred firmly around Hogmanay.

The celebrations of Christmas now fashionable were, of course, invented in the Victorian era, with the customs observed today being drawn largely from the influence of Victoria and Albert who, with their base at Balmoral, held some sway over Scottish social mores. Certain of their customs, largely English in origin, took hold in parts of Scotland; Christmas cards were even invented in Edinburgh in the mid-nineteenth century. The adoption of

Christmas festivities from south of the border continued, especially from the 1960s onwards, and now the Scots celebrate Christmas with as much enthusiasm and excess as the rest of Christendom.

Hogmanay

Possibly the traditional celebration most associated with the Scots although, in a reciprocal swopping over of traditional end-of-year festivities, the New Year has recently come to be welcomed with increased enthusiasm south of the border, too.

An important and symbolic task to be completed on Hogmanay is the cleaning of the whole house and taking care of any outstanding chores. Although this has recently become less widespread, it is still considered unlucky in many areas to go into the New Year with unfinished business from the old year.

First Footing

After 'the bells', as the ringing in of the New Year at midnight is known, it is common for Scots to go out visiting family and friends. The first visitor after the bells on New Year's Day, or Ne'er Day, as it used to be called, is known as the 'first foot', and they can affect the luck that the household will have for the coming year.

The preferred first foot to bring good luck on a house for the forthcoming twelve months (as well as some temporary aesthetic diversion to its mistress after her hard day's cleaning) is a tall, dark man. He should bring symbolic gifts of coal, shortbread or black bun (a heavily spiced Scottish cake) and salt as tokens of prosperity and health

Traditional first-foot gifts

for the year to come. Whisky or some other alcohol is usually brought too.

However, the wrong first foot could have the opposite effect, bringing bad luck. A man with eyebrows meeting in the middle or with flat feet was unlucky, but the worst scenario was a red-haired female first foot. The only way to avoid the misfortune that would certainly follow this was to throw a pinch of salt into the fire immediately.

Other Customs

Part of the Hogmanay tradition still found in some parts of Scotland was the opening of doors and windows in the house, regardless of the January chill. This represented letting the Old Year out, and admitting the New Year. This custom was often accompanied by lots of noise: bells being rung, pots banging and people shouting were not just signs of exuberant celebration, they were also intended to scare away any malign influences that could have gathered over the previous twelve months.

Part of the New Year celebration at midnight is the singing of *Auld Lang Syne*. This has become a tradition in Scotland over the last two centuries, and it is customary for the company to come together into a circle, crossing arms across their fronts to hold hands with the people on either side, for what can often be a very boisterous rendition.

New Year is seen in Scotland as a time of great good-will, and most Scots enter willingly into the festivities. It has always been customary to share in communal celebrations at this time of year, and this continues to happen across the country, even in the cities where many other traditions have long since died. In recent years, larger number than ever have braved the Hogmanay weather to join the festivities in Princes Street in Edinburgh and at Glasgow Cross. Complete strangers happily approach each other after midnight to wish one another a 'Happy New Year', and men and women exchange a kiss.

Fire Festivals

Dating from Pagan times, fire festivals were intended to ward off the evil spirits who might have grasped their chance to work their wicked magic on the darkest and shortest days of the year. Fire was revered by the pagan Celts as the closest thing on earth to the sun, which they worshiped as the giver of life. The many fire festivals held across Scotland were intended to honour the sun, and encourage it to return and bring new life after winter.

Burning the Clavie

This ancient festival in Burghead, Morayshire, takes place every year on 11th January – New Year's Eve, until the calendar was changed in 1582. According to some local traditions, Burning the Clavie dates back to pagan times, but its origins are not clear.

The proceedings get under way when the townspeople make themselves large torches, which they set alight. They then process round the harbour, cleansing the fishing boats of any malign influences.

The Clavie itself is a barrel or similar, filled with tar and other flammable materials and which is then lit. It is carried around the town on a long pole by the Clavie King. He carries it to the top of a local hill, where it is set on a pillar called the Clavie Stone and left to burn out. Embers from the fire are traditionally coveted by the locals as they are thought to bring good luck for the year, in exactly the same way that embers from the Beltane fires used to be sought-after centuries ago.

Flambeaux Procession

The village of Comrie in Perthshire holds a spectacular torchlight procession on Hogmanay. Huge torches are prepared and set on poles, up to ten feet long. On the stroke of midnight they are lit and carried through the streets to the accompaniment of bagpipes. The villagers then return to the square, where their torches are tossed together into a giant bonfire.

Stonehaven

Similar to the Comrie Flambeaux Procession, the spectacular fireball procession in Stonehaven also takes place on 31st December. Large, completely spherical fireballs are made and are set alight on the stroke of midnight. Then, with a display of bravado to make a firefighter wince, the bearers process through the streets swinging the flaming balls around their heads.

It is unclear exactly why this death-defying feat is performed. The fireball may be representative of the sun, with the swinging motion mimicking the sun's passage through the sky. But the ritual is also similar to that performed by the children of Lanark at Whuppity Stourie (see p. 93), where whirling an orb around the head is intended to scare off evil forces.

Other Winter Festivals

The Ba' Game

Kirkwall on the island of Orkney hosts a traditional game of street football on the first day of the New Year. Its origins are unclear, but according to local legend it began during the island's period of Norse rule.

The Ba' Game is played between rival teams from opposite ends of the town. The teams come together on the kirk green and the game begins. There are no obvious rules or regulations, and the game is over when one side has succeeded in driving the other into their side of the town.

Handsel Monday

Handsel Monday was the first Monday after the old New Year's Day on 11th January, and was a recognised holiday in Scotland for workers and labourers. It survived as a separate holiday until its cancellation in the late-nineteenth century.

'Handsel' was the old Scots word for a gift or tip, and workers would receive extra money from their employers, much as English workers did on Boxing Day. The last Handsel Monday Holiday in Scotland was in Dunfermline.

Burns' Suppers

25th January (the date of Robert Burns' birth in 1759) is when Scots and would-be Scots at home and all over the world celebrate the remarkable life and work of the poet through song, poetry, food and drink – no doubt as Burns himself would have chosen to be remembered.

Although the poet had been celebrated in a fairly haphazard fashion since his death, it was only with the centenary of his birth in 1859 that the Burns Supper as we now know it came into being.

The evening formerly tended to be an exclusively male affair (with the exception of the waiting staff), although this is rarely the case now. The menu, however, has not changed: the centrepiece of the meal is the haggis, object of mystery to most non-Scots (and even fear to some), and the subject of one of Burns' best-known works, *Address to the Haggis*. (See p. 122.) It is brought into the dining room accompanied by a playing piper and is ceremonially cut open.

The haggis is then served with neeps and tatties, Scottish soul food for the long winter's evening. The meal is accompanied by another of Burns' great loves, plenty of whisky, to be raised and downed several times for the many toasts of the night, including one to the poet's 'Immortal Memory', and another 'To the Lassies'. The celebration usually ends with more recitals of the great poet's works.

Up Helly-Aa

Arguably the finest fire festival existing in Europe, Up Helly-Aa takes place in Lerwick in the Shetland Islands on the last Tuesday in January, probably originally in celebration of the end of the ancient Yule festival. It also recognises the islands' traditional heritage and culture as part of the Norse lands, rather than Scotland.

A locally made Viking longboat, complete with figurehead, is paraded through the streets of Lerwick by hundreds of Shetlanders in Viking dress. These Vikings go by the name of 'guisers', an echo of the traditional Scots name for Hallowe'en masquers. As darkness falls, the ship is taken to the river as part of a torchlight procession, and is set alight. After the galley has been burned, the rest of the night is spent in drinking, dancing and revelry until dawn.

Up Helly-Aa is one of the few traditional events left in Scotland which continues to thrive and grow: although still very much a local festival, and one for which participants can spend months preparing, it can also draw its 'Vikings' from as far afield as Australia. It also attracts many tourists as spectators, drawn by the fun as well as the sense of drama and the spectacle. A spectacle of a different kind can be seen in Lerwick next morning, as pedestrians step warily over the occasional, now-senseless Viking lying, helmet askew, in the gutter.

Jedburgh Ba' Games

There are two traditional ball games played in this Border town before the start of Lent. The Lads' Ba' Game, which is also known as the Callants' Ba' Game, is traditionally played by the local schoolboys on 2nd February, Candlemas Day. The Men's Ba' Game follows on Fastern's E'en. This is an old Scots name for Shrove Tuesday, which was a day of feast and preparation before the time of fasting and abstinence during Lent.

A form of hand ball, the Ba' Game is extremely vigorous and strenuous although more restrained than it used to be. In 1704, the Town Council banned the football aspect of it, as it was felt to be so violent that lives could be in danger.

The teams are known as the Uppies and the Doonies, depending on the side of town the players come from. They gather in the market place and at 2pm, the first ball is thrown into the air. The two teams then jostle for the ball, trying to grab it by the attached ribbons. Whoever gets a hold of it then tries to run, but the end result is usually the same – both teams end up in the river.

The game was prohibited in the 1840s, again for being too rowdy, but by appealing to the High Court in

Jedburgh Ba' Game

Edinburgh, the right to play the game in the streets of the town was 'sanctioned by immemorial usage'.

In a town so close to the border with England, and consequently with a history which was often violent, local legends can be extremely colourful. According to one tale, the Men's Ba' Game originated as an excuse for the local men to hold an apparently innocuous gathering, which was actually a cover for a nocturnal raid over the border. In another wonderfully gruesome version of the story, the game is said to be based on the conduct of some victorious Scots with the severed heads of their defeated English enemies after a local battle.

But while this story may entertain the tourists, these ancient ball games have actually been played for many centuries. Similar sports are found in communities across the country, including Berwickshire and Perthshire, and there was also an exclusively female version in Musselburgh, where the two teams comprised married and single women.

◆ Spring ◆ ◆

Whuppity Stourie

This celebration of spring is held in Lanark on the first day of March, and may well have originated in an ancient rite to welcome the new season.

Whuppity Stourie, or its variation, Whuppity Scourie, was the name of a bad fairy, and this event, with all its running around, bell-ringing and noise, was to scare off this and any other malign influences that might be around to threaten the start of spring, and the period of growth and prosperity it represented. The ritual is based in the ancient belief that evil fairies could travel in clouds of dust, known in Scotland as 'stour' (pronounced 'stoor'), and would fly around the area blighting crops and cursing animals.

As the festival is practiced nowadays, local children gather in front of the church, waiting for the time to reach exactly six o'clock in the evening. At that moment, the church bells are rung for what is the first time in six months to mark the arrival of spring. This signal starts a race around the building, with each child carrying a paper ball with streamers attached, which are used to whirl it round their heads and hit others as they run. After three circuits a scramble or scatter (see p. 50) is provided for the children, which is followed by a short address from the Provost.

In the past, the ritual was rather more violent, with youths rather than children as participants. They often ended up in confrontation with their local counterparts from New Lanark. A celebratory rhyme reflected the tone of the event, although the third line would change depending on whether Old or New Lanark were the victors:

> Hooray, boys, hooray!
> For we hae won the day:
> We've met the bold New Lanark boys,
> And chased them down the brae!

Lanark's Whuppity Stourie has clear parallels with the Hogmanay fireball procession in Stonehaven. The traditional New Year cleaning of the house to remove evil spirits is instead the spring clean, while the same bell-ringing, ball-whirling rites are performed to scare off malign forces.

Hunt the Gowk

As in all other parts of Britain, April the First is a day of jokes and good-natured trickery. The Anglicised version of 'All Fools' Day' seems to have caught on in recent years, but the day was traditionally known in Scotland as 'Hunt the Gowk'. 'Gowk' was the old Scottish word meaning both 'fool' and 'cuckoo' – the appearance of a cuckoo was seen as one of the first signs of spring's arrival.

Although the English title implies that the custom lasts all day, it is acknowledged that jokes must only be played in the morning, between dawn and midday, and any over-enthusiastic prankster who tries to carry the fun on into the afternoon automatically becomes the Gowk themselves.

Easter

Egg-rolling at Easter was common in areas of northern England and Ireland, but it was especially so in Scotland, where it was considered symbolic of the luck to follow in the coming year.

In the Hebrides, for example, each egg was marked with its owner's identifying sign before being rolled downhill. If it reached the bottom in one piece, good luck would follow for its roller throughout the coming year but, with the usual stroke of the double-edged sword in these matters, misfortune would surely follow if it broke.

The tradition of egg-rolling is very ancient and pre-dates the Christian festival of Easter. The ancient Celts saw the egg as analogous with spring, with new life springing from an apparently dormant environment.

Kate Kennedy

Every April, the students of St Andrews University stage a costume procession named after Kate Kennedy, which sees around a hundred students dress as characters from both local and Scottish history. They are followed in a carriage by the young man dressed as Kate Kennedy, with 'her' entourage. Participation in the event by real females is not allowed, as the event is organised and performed exclusively by male students.

According the local stories, Kate was the niece of a local bishop. Some reports claim she visited St Andrews in the fifteenth century, and her beauty and charm made her the toast of the town. Less romantic accounts place the origin of the event in the 1840s, when it may have been a student 'rag' that caught on. Whatever the true date of the procession's origins, it is still not clear either how Kate Kennedy came to be associated with it, nor why she and her entourage should still be represented by men who want to dress as women.

Beltane

This festival, now more commonly known as May Day, was one of the most important times in the pagan Celtic year, and its celebration is an ancient custom.

On the eve of Beltane, all domestic fires were extinguished, and local people would gather round the hilltop bonfires that were the centrepiece of the ceremonies. The fires would be lit at sunset then watched until dawn. Embers from the dying fires were gathered by all those who attended and taken home where they were used to relight the fire. This would not be completely extinguished again until next Beltane eve, bringing blessings on the house.

Together with the sun, represented by fire, water was the other vital component revered by the Celts for its part in creating life. At dawn on Beltane morning, the Druids would collect the May dew. Believed to have considerable powers, the dew was used in sacred Celtic rituals. There still exists in some parts of Scotland a superstitious belief that washing one's face in the dawn May dew brings good luck and beauty for the next year.

This custom was kept alive right up to modern times in the country, with Beltane celebrations in Perthshire, Aberdeenshire and Shetland carrying on into the nineteenth century. And in recent years Beltane celebrations have undergone a revival across the country. One of the most important fires nowadays is lit on Calton Hill in Edinburgh, where large crowds assemble on the eve of Beltane for their own fire festival, with contemporary entertainment and re-enactments of centuries-old pagan rituals.

◆ Summer ◆ ◆

The Scots take advantage of any good weather available by packing lots of outdoor events into the summer months.

Fire Festivals

Until relatively recently the all-year tradition of Scottish fire festivals was continued in Durris, in Deeside, where a midsummer fire was traditionally burnt. F. Marian McNeill describes it: 'The only place in Scotland where the Midsummer Fire appears to have burned without interruption from prehistoric times until the middle of the present century is the Deeside parish of Durris.' The fire continued for so long thanks to a 1787 bequest by Alexander Hogg, a local man who had helped with the ritual as a child before moving away and making his fortune. He never forgot the fire festival and wanted it to continue for future generations. The ceremony was stopped only in 1939, with the onset of the Second World War.

These midsummer festivals were very probably held in other parts of the country and were similar to the Beltane celebrations. With the advent of Christianity, some of the pagan traditions associated with midsummer were again appropriated by the new church as the feast of St John the Baptist. This integration of pagan beliefs into Christian teachings could lead to some fairly confused beliefs, and this is well illustrated in parts of north-eastern Scotland, where a piece of St John's Wort, picked on St John's Eve, was placed under the pillow at night so the saint would appear to the sleeper and bless them for the coming year.

Gala Days

Most of the summer festivities in Scotland are not quite so steeped in myth as the fire festivals. Towns and villages all over the country have a gala day, when the people get together, usually at a local green or church.

A Gala Queen is chosen from the local schoolgirls, and is crowned for the day to preside over events. There are normally sporting events and competitions for the crowd to join in, with stalls offering games and penny-gambling.

The format is the same in most parts of the country, but some of these festivals have local names to commemorate events in the community's past. The festival of the Herring Queen at the port of Eyemouth in Berwickshire celebrates the fishing industry, while the Marymass Fair in Irvine supposedly commemorates the landing there in 1563 of Mary, Queen of Scots.

Glasgow Fair

After the consecration of Glasgow Cathedral in the 1190s, King William I, the Lion, announced a great fair to celebrate the inauguration of the church. It was to be held over eight days in July, the octave of the Apostles Peter and Paul. What became the Glasgow Fair has been celebrated each July since then for eight hundred years.

Although it was originally part-market, this aspect of the event declined in the eighteenth century and it became dominated by popular entertainers, including freak shows and circuses, in the process proving a huge attraction for local thieves and beggars as well as people from the surrounding areas. It increased in size to the extent that local people protested in the 1840s as the Fair gradually spread out to take over the greater part of the city centre.

After the Second World War, the week's holiday became a fortnight and nowadays, 'the Fair' is generally understood to mean the last two weeks in July – the time when most of Glasgow takes its summer holiday. One of the sites for the original Fair, and the location chosen for the event's short-lived revival in the 1990s, was Glasgow Green, a large expanse of common land on the banks of the Clyde close to the city centre, where Glaswegians still enjoy the right freely to graze their cows and sheep.

The Border Ridings

The Borders between Scotland and England – now a thin imaginary line which can, in signposted places, be straddled by photo-conscious tourists – actually took many centuries to become as firmly established as they are today. In medieval times, when the area – then known as the Marches – was in a state of flux, the people of the Border towns would regularly patrol their southern or northern boundaries in an attempt to enforce them and discourage their neighbours on the other side from any thoughts of encroachment.

Riding the Marches, as it came to be known, is a custom of great antiquity and is still ceremoniously performed in several of the Border towns, including Galashiels, Hawick, Selkirk and Melrose. These festivals take place throughout the summer months, and can last anywhere between a two or three days and several weeks.

The festivities are often led by a local man, who is the standard bearer and who leads the cavalcade. He has a different name in each area – in Hawick, he is known as

Riding the Marches

the Coronet; in Galashiels, the Braw Lad – and is accompanied by a female consort. They preside over the events, which usually include games, processions and equestrian shows or competitions.

Most of the Ridings include a number of minor ridings and one major event, which symbolises the town laying claim to the ownership of common land. Although most of these ceremonies have the same roots, each one has its own peculiarities. The Hawick Riding is slightly different, based on a local battle in 1514, the year after many of the townsmen had fallen at the Battle of Flodden. News of approaching English marauders was met with dismay as there were so few men left to defend the town. The local youths banded together and set out to meet the enemy, surprising them at Hornshole where the English forces were routed and their flag captured. A replica of this standard, known as the Hexham Pennant, still figures in the town's ridings.

In recent years the male-only Hawick ridings became the focus of media attention after some fairly unpleasant scenes when local women who wanted to take part were met with abuse and violence. However, the combination of bad publicity and human-rights legislation have ensured that a more even-handed approach will follow for all who want to join in what are supposed to be enjoyable events.

Lanimer Day

Away from the Border country, a very similar ceremony is held in Lanark, county town of the old burgh of Lanarkshire. Lanimer Day, celebrated annually in early June, begins with the Lord Coronet leading a procession and ride around the boundaries. This is followed by more typical Gala Day celebrations, presided over by the Lanimer Queen. Locals claim the pageant has been held since 1140, when Lanark received its burgh charter.

The Burryman and Ferry Fair

For hundreds of years, South Queensferry's annual fair has been held in the second week of August. The first stage of the event actually takes place on the day before the Fair, with the procession of the Burryman.

Whichever local man takes on the role of the Burryman must spend several hours preparing his costume. First he is dressed from head to foot in flannel, with holes cut out at the head for him to see through. Next comes the coat of sticky burrs that give him his name. These have been prepared in advance to form a thick coat that covers him

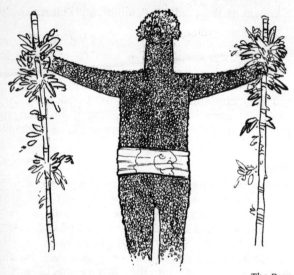

The Burryman

completely, and his fantastic ensemble is finished off with a large hat topped with flowers.

The Burryman is then guided round town by two attendants who also collect donations from bystanders. If the Burryman decides to enter any building, he is thought to bestow good luck on its inhabitants. His parade continues until early evening, when he can at last take off the heavy suit.

The Ferry Fair proper is held the next day, with the same sort of amusements, entertainments and side-shows as most other local fairs and gala days. Presided over by the

Ferry Queen, a local schoolgirl, the day is mostly taken up with races followed by a fun fair.

Highland Games

Despite their name, these events are not just confined to the Highlands, but take place across the country in the summer months. A mix of sports-meeting and entertainment, they would have given clan chiefs a chance to assess the skills of their men in times past. Now they are more commercial, and competitors travel from different parts of the world to compete in their traditional events: tossing the caber, throwing the hammer and Highland dancing.

The royal family has its own tradition of attending Highland Games. Since 1848, when Queen Victoria first attended the Braemar Gathering, there have been royal spectators in the crowd there if the family are in residence at Balmoral.

Tossing the caber

103

Residents of the town of Ceres in Fife have traditionally claimed to hold the oldest Highland Games in Scotland. The games formed part of a Midsummer Festival established in 1314 by the men of Ceres, to mark their triumphant return from the Battle of Bannockburn.

◆ Autumn ◆ ◆

Hallowe'en

The Christian festival of the Eve of All Hallows was set deliberately on 31st October so that it would coincide with the already existing and ancient Celtic festival of Samhain. Bonfires were traditionally lit all over the country on that date although these are not now so common, having moved over the last hundred years to Guy Fawkes Night on 5th November, which has come to be popularly known as Bonfire Night. Other old customs from the traditional celebrations have survived better.

Traditionally, Scots children go guising: dressed in fancy dress, they visit neighbouring houses where they sing a song, recite a poem or tell jokes for a reward of apples, nuts or sweets – and, in increasingly materialistic times, for money. In earlier times, guising was as popular among adults as children, with people dressing as spirits to represent the dead or the other uncanny beings who were believed to be abroad. In some parts of the country, people blackened their faces, just as the ancient Druids were thought to have smeared their faces with ashes from the sacred Samhain bonfire.

American influence seems to be overtaking the custom-

Dooking for apples

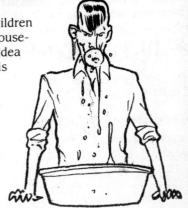

ary practices of the children 'doing a turn' for the household, however, as the idea of 'trick or treat' is catching on. The old Scottish custom of dooking for apples, however, is still popular. A bucket, basin or similar container is filled with water, and apples are floated in it. The object of the game is for each player to remove an apple from the water with their teeth – no hands allowed.

Lanterns made out of hollowed-out turnips (or swedes) containing a candle which shines through a scary face carved into the front, can still be found. But these also seem increasingly discarded in favour of the more North American-flavoured (and easier-to-carve) pumpkin version. Such lanterns seemed to serve much the same purpose as the traditional bonfire, helping to scare off any dark supernatural beings that might be hanging about.

St Andrew's Day

Scotland's patron saint is commemorated on November 30th, a day celebrated with dinners of traditional Scots dishes and toasts to St Andrew and Scotland. It is considered an important date by many Scots living outside the country, giving them a focus for a celebration of their homeland. (see ch. 9.)

◆ All-Year Celebrations ◆ ◆

Dance

Traditional Dancing

Several styles of traditional dancing are recognised in Scotland, reflecting various strands and traditions. The foremost for competition purposes are Highland and Scottish Country Dancing. The old Scottish dances are a mixture of ancient native dances and more recent variants that have evolved, although the roots and meanings of most are long since lost. Increasingly now, however, most are modern in origin, as befits a living and active tradition.

The Ceilidh

For hundreds of years the ceilidh was the traditional Scottish celebration of any event, characterised by dancing, drinking and story-telling late into the night. In Gaelic, 'ceilidh' translates as 'social visit' and it extended to all sorts of informal musical gatherings, whether Gaelic or not.

Together with many other traditions, the ceilidh fell from favour in the twentieth century, but it has recently undergone a revival in fashion and popularity to become again the main form of entertainment at many weddings, parties and other celebrations. The modern version concentrates on drinking and dancing to the popular jigs, waltzes and reels in a spirit of enthusiasm, controlled mayhem and downright fun. The exuberance and merriment of a ceilidh is always, of course, unknown to and undreamt of by the generations of awkward Scots adolescents who are invariably forced, under duress and with great embarrassment, to learn the traditional dances while still at school.

Modern Festivals

While many of Scotland's traditional festivals and customs have been allowed to die out or been forgotten, Scotland's living and evolving culture has seen new celebrations develop, often with the backing of official organisation, to reflect changing national attitudes and priorities. A great number of these are based in and around the more populous cities, but other towns have their own vibrant arts and music festivals, including Inverness, Perth, Aberdeen and Orkney.

Edinburgh Festival

The largest and most famous of Scotland's organised festivals is the Edinburgh International Festival. This celebration of entertainment and the arts began in 1947 to lighten the gloom of austerity in post-war Britain, and still takes place every year over the last three weeks in August.

Ever-expanding in size and reputation, the Edinburgh Festival has now become the biggest arts event of its kind in Europe, and attracts performers and audiences from all over the world. Alongside the official Festival runs the now-equally famous Fringe, the International Film festival, the Book festival and the Military Tattoo.

Music

Song has always been a major element of Scotland's cultural heritage, and folk music is still a strong tradition in many parts of the country. Folk festivals are regular and popular events in many communities.

The Mod

One of the most important music festivals is the National Mod. 'Mod' is a Gaelic word for a gathering, and the first one was organised in Oban in 1892 by An Comunn Gaidhealach, the Highland Association. This competitive celebration of Gaelic music, language and drama has been held annually ever since, moving to a different location around the country each year. It attracts entrants from all parts of Scotland as well as overseas, and has spawned smaller, local mods. Its continued popularity even among non-Gaelic speakers illustrates the lasting appeal the Gaelic culture and its traditions hold for large sections of Scottish society.

5: *Food and Drink*

From earliest times to the present day, food and drink have been central not only to almost all major life events in Scotland, but to any social gathering, right down to the most mundane. Preparing, presenting and consuming food and drink is about much more than simply taking in some nourishment: cultures all over the world use the rituals of food and drink as a way of expressing their care and love; as a means of rewarding; to display piety; or to signify social standing and wealth.

Eating and drinking are integral to Scottish celebrations, and all rites of passage are marked by indulgence (which occasionally proceeds to over-indulgence) in both. Births and christenings, weddings, deaths; the passing of the seasons at Hallowe'en, Hogmanay and Beltane; the religious festivals of Christmas and Easter: each have particular associations with specific foods or dishes. Traditional Scottish foods or dishes for these feasts include Black Bun, the rich fruit cake eaten at Hogmanay and New Year; haggis at Burns' Night; puddings at

Christmas; and pancakes at Fastern's E'en (as Shrove Tuesday was commonly known in Scotland). Special cakes and puddings were also made at Hallowe'en. This magical time was an auspicious time to predict a future partner, and traditional Hallowe'en cake contained charms that would help: for example, whoever found the ring would be first to marry; a coin meant fortune would follow; and a horseshoe signified good luck.

◆ Religious Significance ◆ ◆

Food was a key part of the religion of pre-Christian Scotland. The Druids, who led the main pagan cult, made offerings to appease and give thanks to the gods of nature who were believed to set the rhythms of the earth. Many of the customs practised at festivals in Scotland until relatively recently involved using food as a representative for ritual sacrifice; in earlier times, this may even have been human sacrifice.

Pre-Christian Celebrations

At Beltane fire festivals in the Highlands in the eighteenth century, a large oatcake was made and broken up into as many pieces as there were revellers. One piece was blackened in the fire and was placed in a bag with all the others. Those present had to chose one while blindfolded, and the person who picked out the black piece had to jump three times through the flames. But, unpleasant as it might have been for the jumper, the act was merely symbolic of the burning which would have befallen them centuries before!

In Perthshire and other parts of the north east, a Beltane caudle was made. This was a type of custard containing eggs, milk and oatmeal; a share was poured on the ground, as the blood of the sacrificial offering would have been in times past, and the rest was divided among the company.

Water also had a great deal of significance in religious rituals. As fundamental a part of the natural process of birth and renewal as sunlight, it was regarded with as much reverence by the Druids. In pre-Christian times there were an estimated 600 sites of sacred wells across Scotland. The dew gathered at Beltane was particularly sacred (see p. 96), and water is also a vital part of the Christian ceremony of baptism.

Christian Celebrations

Even after the arrival of Christianity, food continued to be vital to religious practices. The new Church adopted the pagan practice of egg-rolling. The egg was originally a symbol of rebirth and was rolled to mimic the movement of the sun, but for early Christians the egg came to represent the stone rolling away from Christ's tomb at the Resurrection.

From the celebration of the Last Supper to the practice of fasting during the period of Lent, the use of food has been symbolic. Most importantly, it is central in the celebration and commemoration of Christ's sacrifice in the use of bread and wine as a host for, or representation of, Christ's body and blood, according to particular Christian belief.

The feast of St Andrew, Scotland's patron saint, on 30th

November is marked by the eating and drinking of traditional food and drink. This has been an evening of festivity and conviviality for Scots at home and abroad for hundreds of years. The court of King James IV in the early sixteenth century celebrated with a banquet featuring some very familiar fare: venison, wild fowl, spiced puddings and wine – much the same sort of food and drink that is eaten on the feast day today. More modern menus for the evening have also included sheep's head and haggis.

◆ **Attitudes to Food and Drink** ◆ ◆

Gratitude and Grace

Food was traditionally regarded as a gift from God, and one which was acknowledged with gratitude by most diners. Eating a meal without the ceremonial saying of grace would have been unthinkable in most Scottish households, and although it is a practice now only of the com-

Saying grace

mittedly religious, this used to be the standard start to mealtimes in traditional Scots homes.

Despite falling into disuse, many of these old graces are still well-known in their own right. The most famous of them is the so-called Selkirk Grace. It acquired its name after it was spoken by Robert Burns when he was dining with the Earl of Selkirk, but its other name, the Covenanters' Grace, suggests it is older:

> Some hae meat and canna eat,
> And some wad eat that want it;
> But we hae meat and we can eat,
> And sae the Lord be thankit.

Grace was not only said before meals, it could also be said after eating as a form of thanks. Queen Margaret, who was canonised for her piety, introduced the 'grace cup' to the tables of the Scottish court. She wished the diners to stay at the table until the meal was over to give thanks for the food they had received, and she encouraged them to do so by keeping a cup of the best wine to be passed around at the very end of the meal, after the saying of grace.

Hospitality

The traditional hospitality to be found in Scottish homes was once renowned all over the world, and the generosity of the people of the Highlands was especially notable, as the poet Robert Burns described after a trip to the north in 1787:

When death's dark stream I'll ferry o'er –
A time that surely shall come –
In heaven itself I'll ask no more
Than just a Highland welcome.

Sir Richard Sullivan, an Irishman visiting Scotland a few years earlier, had expressed the same sentiments in his letters home: 'Much as we had heard of Scots hospitality, we did not conceive that it could ever have been carried to the extreme in which we found it.'

The Scots took pride in offering the best of whatever they had to visitors, whether known to them or not. This is attitude is expressed through the old Gaelic proverb which translates as, 'Often, often, often, goes the Christ in stranger's guise.' (Incidentally, the violation of this tradition of open-handed hospitality in 1692 was part of the reason why the massacre of the Macdonalds at Glencoe by their guests, the Campbells, was held to be so shocking.) Offering such hospitality was a matter of honour and would-be hosts would frequently fall to squabbling amongst themselves over who should provide a meal and a bed for a traveller.

Life was harsh in many parts of the Highlands, and in such deprivation, gifts in kind like food, drink and accommodation were a means of expressing welcome and giving thanks. An illuminating anecdote has two Highlanders discussing a neighbour. One has nothing good to say about him, and when the other asks why, the response is, 'He was pouring me a glass of whisky and when I said "Stop" – would you believe it – he did!' To be considered mean-spirited or grudging in such a way was a terrible shame, and a great insult if the accusation was unjust.

Such attitudes were also intrinsic to the extended family support of the clan system, where hosting large meals and giving board to unknown relatives from far-flung parts of the country were everyday events. This way of life and hospitality began to fall into decline after the Jacobite Risings. The Clearances of people from the land changed the Scottish Highlands completely, as working on the land was no longer permitted as an economically viable way of life.

Frugality and Excess

The stereotype of the canny, puritanical Scot is a post-Reformation image that not only dies hard, but sits apparently uncomfortably alongside the other traditional depiction of a nation of hard, sly and hypocritical drinkers; both, of course, reflect some degree of reality, distorted or otherwise.

The new Church of Scotland's strict enforcement of the Sabbath after the Reformation of 1560 had an impact on the nation's eating and drinking habits. There were to be no taverns, no brewing of ale, and no baking bread on Sunday. Frugality, previously a virtue forced on people out of necessity, was elevated to the status of righteous and godly living. Over-indulgence at the table or fuss at mealtimes was very much frowned upon. While this is much less common now, it is an outlook that continues to be found in some areas of the Highlands, where the old Scottish proverbs still hold sway: 'Surfeit slays mair than swords'.

Of course, such frugality could be seen as a disdainful attitude to plain food which is exactly opposite to a welcoming embrace of drink. And alcohol has always played a central part in Scottish life. From birth to death and everything in between, traditional celebrations of all occasions in Scotland have alcohol as a key feature.

The painful and all-too-familiar consequences that follow from this approach were described by the writer James Boswell after a particularly heavy night in Skye: 'We were cordial and merry to a high degree; but of what passed I have no recollection with any accuracy ... It was near five in the morning when I got to bed. I awakened at noon, with a severe headache.'

Even today, drinking habits in some island parts of Scotland reflect this combination of frugality and excess: a total abstinence from Sunday to Thursday goes together with a truly phenomenal capacity for drink, which would fell the unpractised, at weekends. The fundamentalist virtues of self-denial can only last so long before they explode in an orgy of over-indulgence, and both are different sides of the same coin.

◆ Scottish Drink ◆ ◆

The first recorded alcoholic drink produced in Scotland was ale, and its popularity has continued right up to the present day as many 'real ales', made using traditional brewing methods, have become fashionable.

In spite of a long history of brewing and drinking ale, it was the drink that was first emerged around a thousand years later that was to become utterly dominant among Scottish drinks, to such a massive degree that it is known around the world simply as 'Scotch'.

Whisky

Aqua vitae, the Latin words for 'water of life', first made their appearance in Scottish state records in the fifteenth century, but it was over a hundred years later that the Gaelic version, *uisge beatha*, replaced them in official terminology. The name was anglicised to give the 'whisky' known all over the world today. In 1736, an exciseman described the benefits of whisky-drinking for the people of the Highlands:

> 'The ruddy complexion, nimbleness and strength of these people is not owing to water-drinking, but to the *aqua vitae*, a malt spirit which is commonly used in that country.'

Belief in the restorative and health-giving powers of the drink is still common, illustrated most popularly in the administering of a hot toddy to those suffering from a cold.

Ales

Although whisky has long been considered Scotland's national drink, the earliest-recorded alcoholic drink was heather ale, which supposedly originated with the Picts. The ale was made of the tops of young heather, boiled and fermented with a few hops and some honey. With mechanisation and standardisation of the brewing industry this very local drink had almost disappeared, but the recent renewal of interest in ancient recipes has resulted in its surprise revival, albeit as an idiosyncratic local beer with novelty value.

Wine

From at least the twelfth century, and up to the eighteenth, Scotland was a huge importer and consumer of French wines, and especially claret, described as the life-blood of the Auld Alliance. This alliance was Scotland's close relationship with France, which had as one of its spin-offs a great influence on traditional Scottish fare. It turned Edinburgh into a wine connoisseurs' capital, which was reputed to have more discriminating taste in wine than any city outside France itself. Claret was for long the favourite French drink of Scotland, and was a standard on wealthier Scottish tables, although it was also available to the lower social classes. Until bottling was introduced in the eighteenth century, claret was dispensed to Edinburgh citizens from the back of a horse-drawn cart for sixpence a jug. The French influence at the table extended to food, too, as can be seen on page 127.

Toasts

A country with such a fondness for drinking obviously should have a wide repertoire of toasts. The origin of toasts dates back a long way and probably stems from drinking to the gods to thank them for providing the alcohol, a practice common to many pre-Christian cultures. Toasts were particularly fashionable in Scotland during the eighteenth and early nineteenth centuries: at a banquet in Edinburgh in honour of George IV's visit in 1822, forty-seven different toasts were drunk to the king. A popular toast still in use today originates in this period:

> Here's tae us;
> Wha's like us?
> Damn few, and they're a' deid.

('Here's to us; who's like us? Damn few and they're all dead'.) The most common traditional toast still used throughout the country today is a Gaelic one, even in areas where the drinkers know no other words of the language: 'Slainte mhor!' – 'Your good health!' Another highly theatrical Gaelic toast should be delivered standing on a chair, with one foot on the table. After proclaiming the toast, the drink should be downed in one and the glass smashed.

One particular group traditionally had their own set of toasts whose wording was known only to themselves. The Jacobites, followers of the deposed Stuart monarchy, continued to toast the man that they saw as the true king of Scotland. The wording of the toast had to be very precise to avoid betrayal and accusations of treason by any infiltrators who happened to be present. An outside observer would have seen nothing treacherous in their apparently loyal toast 'To the King'; but no-one actually drank until their glass had been passed over a jug of water in a recre-

A Jacobite toast

ation of the more traditional Jacobite toast, 'To the King o'er the water'. Another which was even more obscure and also spiked through with a black humour, was the Jacobite toast, 'To the gentleman in the black velvet waistcoat'. William of Orange, II of Scotland, with his wife Mary, was regarded by the Jacobites as having taken the throne from its rightful occupant, James VII. While out riding, William was thrown from his horse as it fell, sustaining injuries from which he later died. The reason for his horse's stumble was identified as a molehill – the home of the 'gentleman in the black velvet waistcoat'!

◆ Scottish Food ◆ ◆

Few foodstuffs or dishes are regarded as particularly Scottish in the way that whisky is, but some notable exceptions to this rule have entered the country's mythology and culture, and coloured its popular image abroad.

Haggis

Haggis is *the* Scottish food *par excellence*, popularly regarded as the national dish. Its precise origins are unknown but are certainly ancient. Similar sausage-based dishes are found in other countries, including second century Greece, where a haggis-type dish is mentioned by Athanaeus in his writings on contemporary food. What distinguishes the Scottish version is its use of staple local foods such as oatmeal, suet and sheep's offal.

Before the advent of mass-produced food and convenience foods, haggis was made at home, by

Cutting open the haggis

121

hand. The traditional recipe involved the use of several fairly stomach-churning ingredients and procedures, and makes unpleasant and off-putting reading for the squeamish. But only a cook who was tradition-obsessed to the point of derangement would put themselves through such preparation nowadays when there are several superb-quality pre-prepared versions (including a vegetarian one) on the market.

Haggis and Burns

Most haggis is consumed on 25th January, the traditional date for Burns Suppers to celebrate the life and works of the poet. It is usually eaten with mashed potato and neeps – turnip, or swede. (Although widely associated with Scotland, this Burns Supper staple does not have a great pedigree as a Scottish classic, having only arrived from Holland in the early eighteenth century). Haggis is of special significance on these occasions, as one of Burns' best known poems was written in praise of it:

> Fair fa' your honest, sonsie face,
> Great chieftain o' the puddin' race!
> Aboon them a' ye tak' your place,
>> Painch, tripe or thairm;
> Weel are ye worthy of a grace
>> As lang's my airm.
>> (*Address to a Haggis*)

This link between the haggis and the country's national bard has helped keep the dish as part of the national culture, both in Scotland and in all other parts of the world where migrant Scots and their descendants live.

Oatmeal

Oatmeal is now mostly thought of as the basis for haggis and porridge, Scotland's other national dish, which was valued so much by Burns that he described it as 'the halesome parritch, chief o' Scotia's food'. Samuel Johnson, not a fan, defined it as 'a grain which in England is generally given to horses, but in Scotland supports the people', and in his tour of Scotland in the 1770s, he took the precaution of taking his own bread. During a stay in the Highlands in 1818, the poet John Keats must have wished he had shown similar foresight. 'I fell upon a bit of white bread today like a sparrow ... I cannot manage the cursed oatcake,' he wrote in a letter home.

Yet oats have been a staple of Scottish cooking since at least the sixth century due to the relatively harsh agricultural conditions in many areas of the country. Oatmeal is found in a huge number of dishes, including oatcakes and all types of brose. In the past it has been used for many things, from a washing agent to a preservative, and there are reports of meat being kept for weeks after being covered in oatmeal.

Brose

Once described as the core of the Scots peasant diet, brose was originally a mixture of water or milk and oatmeal. On days of special celebration, it would be flavoured with whisky or honey.

The most famous variation on the traditional brose was the one supposed to have been created by the Earl of Atholl and named after him, as Atholl Brose. This mixture of honey, whisky and meal was first recorded in 1475, but may well be considerably older. It is still a favourite with Scottish cooks today, although it normally features as part of the pudding course.

According to legend, it was used by the earl to capture Iain Macdonald, the Lord of the Isles. Macdonald was in the habit of stopping at a well to drink, and the Earl of Atholl filled the well with the brose. Macdonald stopped to drink at the well as usual, but was surprised by the contents. As he delayed his departure to drink more, the Earl's forces were able to creep up and capture him.

An alternative legend, from around a hundred years later, tells of Ruraidh Mor, a wild man who lived in the woods where a young female relative of the Earl of Atholl liked to walk. This savage terrorised and robbed passers by until a young local man filled a nearby well where he was accustomed to drink, with the mixture of honey, whisky and oatmeal. As in the earlier tale, the surprising contents distracted Ruraidh Mor and the young man was able to capture him, winning for himself the hand of the Atholl heiress. In reality, the recipe is probably nothing to do with the family who have given it its name, and a number of brose variations exist. But Atholl Brose is the most common, and was the recipe enjoyed by Queen Victoria during a visit to the Earl of Atholl in 1844.

Mealy Monday

One curious tradition that persevered in Scotland well into the twentieth century was based around oatmeal.

Scottish universities celebrated every February an annual holiday which was known as Mealy Monday. This was intended to give impoverished students the chance to return to their parents' home and restock the large bag of

oatmeal that would then provide the basis for their mea-
gre diet until the next year.

Kail

While oatmeal is still acknowledged as a 'Scottish'
food, a vegetable that used
to be found all over
Scotland, but is now rarely
even heard of, is kail. A sort
of cabbage, kail is a winter
vegetable with a rather
more spicy taste and was
used to add flavour to
soups and brose, as well as
being cooked and served as
part of a meal. While it was

Kail

grown in gardens in all parts of Scotland, it was more
common in lowland areas.

Kail entered into other areas of popular culture and at
Hallowe'en it was common to study the kail roots as a
means of divination. Each member of the party would pull
up a piece of kail, and the shape and size of the roots
would be interpreted to give clues to the appearance and
character of a future partner.

It was at one time so widely and regularly eaten that its
name even became the generic term for a meal. In eigh-
teenth-century Edinburgh, the St Giles Bell which was
rung at two o'clock each day was known as the Kail Bell.
And the term Kailyard School was even used in literature,

applied to a group of writers, including J. M. Barrie, who specialised in homely tales of Scotland at the start of the twentieth century.

Kail's virtual disappearance is mainly due to fashion. As the range of vegetables readily available on Scottish tables increased, the old reliable kail came to be seen as unsophisticated and 'common'; a symbol of lower social status. As 'kailyard' entered the language as a pejorative term, more often than not, the vegetable that gave it its name became more and more unfashionable.

Seaweed

The more common alternative to kail in the Scottish Highlands and islands was seaweed, or sea vegetables, as the many different varieties were sometimes known. One of a number of specifically local foodstuffs, it was used in many ways, including the flavouring of whiskies; its taste can still be discerned in some of the Islay whiskies today.

◆ Scottish Meals ◆ ◆

One source that offers useful information on traditional Scottish foods and diets is the writing of Walter Scott. Obviously a man who enjoyed the table, he gave detailed descriptions of meals.

For Samuel Johnson, the generous and satisfying breakfasts he consumed were particularly appreciated during his time north of the border. 'If an epicure could remove by a wish in quest of sensual gratification, wherever he had supped, he would breakfast in Scotland,' he wrote.

Foreign Influence

The single most obvious outside influence on Scottish cooking came from France, as a result of the cultural ties brought about by the Auld Alliance between the two countries. From the fourteenth century, exiled Scottish families living in France learned both cooking techniques and phrases that then made their way back to the Scottish kitchen. Words like 'gigot' and 'ashet' are still part of the language of Scottish cooking.

Marmalade

The story customarily told to explain the arrival of marmalade in Scotland also concerns the Auld Alliance and one of its key players, Queen Mary.

In 1561 the queen returned to her northern kingdom after the death of her husband, the young king of France. She was said to have brought the orange preserve on board ship to counteract seasickness and, when her maid was asked by a Scottish courtier what the preserve was, she replied without understanding the question: 'Marie est malade'. It would be difficult to miss the connection with the Anglicised name but sadly the story is an apocryphal one.

The first orange marmalade made in Scotland also has an interesting background. In the early eighteenth century, a Spanish ship in difficulties and carrying a cargo of Spanish oranges, docked at Dundee. As the fruit was already over-ripe and would not last, the crew sold them off cheaply and Janet Keiller, a local woman, supposedly persuaded her merchant husband to buy the entire stock. She made them into the preserve that helped spread

Dundee's reputation across the world as Scotland's marmalade capital and the family went on to open the country's first marmalade factory in 1797.

Marmalade is still a key part of the traditional Scottish breakfast that continues to fortify tourists and is the pride of many of the country's small hotels and guesthouses.

6: Witchcraft

Mention the word 'witch' today and visions of women in long, billowing robes with spellbooks, broomsticks, pointy hats and familiars would automatically suggest themselves in many minds. But even as recently as a century and a half ago, before the blessings of modern medicine and the concurrent advances in its practice, witchcraft and the superstitious use of charms as protection were commonplace among the everyday dangers and the uncertainty of life for almost everyone. In such a harsh world where sudden sickness and misfortune were random, often unexpected, usually untreatable and all-too-frequently fatal, a belief in human power over such matters might make them more easy to deal with, if not to control.

◆ Common Powers of a Witch ◆ ◆

A witch was an important figure, whether respected or feared, in any local community. The alternative term of 'wise woman (or man)' is a useful one, suggesting as it does someone with experience and knowledge. This knowledge could manifest itself as healing powers, charms or other secrets which might spring from something as commonplace as a familiarity with plant lore (see ch. 10), folk medicine, a basic knowledge of midwifery or first-aid, or even just the power of others' imagination.

Far from conjuring up spells in league with the Devil, or flying in a magic hat (the supernatural transport of choice in Scotland), witches tended to concentrate their work on the less spectacular and more mundane tasks of providing love potions, divining for lost items, answering specific questions of prophesy or giving herbal or restorative remedies or advice. Some health-giving powers were thought to reside in families, being passed on through the generations: the seventh son of a seventh son was thought able to heal skin diseases like eczema, by touch alone.

Ill-Wishing

There was a widespread belief in the Evil Eye, believed by many in the Highlands to be hereditary and involuntary. Sickness and death, especially in children and animals, were thought to be caused by this. Individuals or even entire families would be feared, or even shunned if they were thought to have this power – it was believed that those who possessed it might harm even their own families or animals involuntarily just by looking at them. Ways to cancel out such ill-wishing included spitting on the ground or accusing the ill-wisher with what she or he had done.

Other, more common and less serious types of ill-wishing included stealing the goodness, or profit, of some types of foods – a farmer's crop, a yield of milk or a fisherman's catch all might be blighted by a witch taking their goodness for herself.

Second Sight

Second sight, like the Evil Eye, was usually considered to be hereditary and an unsought power. This type of clairvoyance usually had something to do with death: whether foretelling someone's death, by some symbolic or literal vision, realising that it had already taken place, or knowing where the dead body of a missing person could be found. But although this was the most dread type, it could also extend to other types of prophesy. Kenneth Mackenzie, or Coinneach Odhar, the legendary Brahan Seer, was thought to have seen a vast number of extraordinary prophesies, from the coming of railways and aeroplanes to the Highland Clearances. Whether or not the Brahan Seer actually existed is now not certain, although an arrest warrant was issued for a witch of his name in the sixteenth century.

Charms

Part of the rituals of everyday life were the precautions and charms people took or wore to ward off ill-luck. These were many and diverse, ranging from customs as simple and familiar as the still-practised not spilling salt or walking under a ladder, to the more specific avoidance of pigs and cats on the way out on a fishing-trip, or the putting of rowan twigs or a Bible in the bed of a woman in childbirth or of a new baby, to ward off the fairies.

◆ Witchcraft and Religion ◆ ◆

In a way that is difficult to comprehend nowadays, these beliefs in the earth-bound supernatural existed easily in tandem with, and often complemented, Christian religious beliefs. Traditional holy wells, of which there were many around the country, were still revered and visited long after the significance or holiness of the sites they stood on was denied. More famously, one particular Scottish priest was an infamous wizard and one of the most famous men in Europe of his day.

Michael Scott

Michael Scott is thought to have been born around 1175 in the Borders, but not much else is known of his early life. According to the legend, he studied Arabic, astronomy and chemistry at the great medieval universities of Oxford, Paris and Padua before going on to study with the Moors, the foremost scientists and mathematicians of the time, at Toledo in Spain. In 1220 he moved to Palermo to join the glittering and learned court of the Emperor Frederick the Great. There he became court astrologer, a position that allowed him to explore his interest in the occult, sorcery and prophesy.

Michael Scott's learning and supposed supernatural powers were known throughout Europe, and his reputation as a fearsome wizard was widespread. He was said to sail in a demon ship, and fly through the air on an invisible horse, allowing him to arrive at the Papal Court in Rome in the summer with new-fallen snow on his cloak, fresh from crossing the Alps. With his powers of prediction, he foretold both the emperor's death and his own demise. He is mentioned in Dante's *Inferno,* one of the enchanters in the eighth circle of Hell. His legend also claims that he was responsible for the division of the Eildon Hills into three while casting one of his spells.

Although Scott did not practice witchcraft in the way it was later interpreted, he was the most prominent wizard of Scottish history. His reception in the highest courts in Europe and the respect he was shown across the continent was in stark contrast to the fate of those accused of similar practices four hundred years later.

The Reformation

In the seventeenth century the cross-over of superstition, witchcraft and religion was a practice which the new, sternly and enthusiastically reformed Church of Scotland was determined to stamp on, as the ministers of the new Kirk brought their particular fervent brand of Christianity, with its literal interpretation of the Bible, into people's lives. Just three years after the Reformation was made official in Scotland, witchcraft was made a crime when Parliament passed a law in 1563, forbidding 'ony maner of witchcraftis, sorsaries or necromancie under pane of deid'.

But Scotland's infamous witch-craze did not really take off until 1590, its flames fanned by no less a person than the king, James VI. Such was his interest that he published his own book on the topic, *Daemonologie,* in 1597, to justify the persecution craze then gripping the country, and

James VI

declaim on the evil of pacts with the Devil. It was James' stay in Denmark in 1590, collecting his new bride, that introduced him to the continental enthusiasm for outing malevolent and Satanic witchcraft, and it was a fashion he wholeheartedly embraced. Almost as soon as he got home, he took personal charge of the trial of a group of witches from North Berwick who were charged with trying, in league with the Devil, to sink the ship which brought him home.

The Witches of North Berwick

The trial began after the Deputy Bailiff of Tranent accused one of his servant girls of witchcraft. Under torture, she confessed and named a number of other people who she claimed were her accomplices.

The Accused

One of those implicated in this confession was Agnes Sampson, a well-educated woman who seems to have been respected in her community. She too was tortured until she confessed to increasingly outrageous offences. These included necromancy, communing with the Devil, and being part of a coven.

The king's particular interest in the case was aroused when Agnes named him as one of her proposed victims, and he elected to interview her himself. She claimed that when James was returning home with his bride, she and the other members of her coven had sailed up the waters of the River Forth at Leith in magic sieves, calling up storms in an attempt to sink his ship. Her evidence was accepted by the king, and Agnes was executed at Haddington in 1591.

Another of those accused was John Fian, a local school master. He was allegedly the Master of the coven, and after being subjected to extreme torture, he too confessed and was executed in the same year.

Acquaintance with some of the significant 'witches' named was enough evidence to implicate Francis Stewart, the Earl of Bothwell and a cousin of the king. Stewart was, coincidentally or not, a vigorous opponent of several of James' policies, a fact which was undoubtedly a further spur to the king's determination. His prosecution of Bothwell was ultimately unsuccessful, but the earl was the subject of speculation and rumour for many years afterwards, and his political credibility was irretrievably damaged as a result.

Aspects of the Trial

The trial of the North Berwick witches had important implications for future prosecutions. It was the first to use sustained torture to extract confessions and names of other supposed witches.

Around seventy people were eventually named over the period of the trials, and many of them were executed, although it is impossible to know the exact number.

◆ Discovering a Witch ◆ ◆

Torture

In addition to the various ordeals suspects were subjected to in an attempt to gather 'evidence' against them, torture was a feature of hundreds of trials. The justification for this brutality was that the Devil's hold on his subjects was very strong, and could often only be broken by extreme pain. This freed the witch of the Devil's influence and allowed her to speak the truth freely.

Sleep deprivation was the first form of torture, followed quickly by 'boots' on the legs, which would gradually crush the bones. A rope was bound round the head and gradually wound tighter; thumb-screws were applied, and fingernails were systematically torn off. In one particularly barbarous example, the torture was not directly applied to the witch. During a 1594 trial on Orkney, the accused was forced to watch her elderly husband and two young children being tortured in an attempt to force a confession from her.

Swimming

A series of trials in Aberdeen in 1596 ended with twenty-four burnings. Accusations levelled against those involved ranged from causing death by the curse of the evil eye to raising storms and bringing on nightmares.

Some of the accused were subjected to ordeals. One of these was 'swimming', which involved the suspects being bound hands to ankles and thrown into deep water. If they floated, it was interpreted as a sign of their guilt – they were obviously being protected by their master, Satan. If they sank, they were considered innocent, although this can have been little consolation for the poor souls who drowned to prove it.

Swimming was used occasionally in Scotland to search out witches, but it was more commonly found in England and other parts of Europe. For Scottish trials, the customary method of detecting a witch was by 'pricking'.

Prickers

Witches were believed to enter into a pact with the Devil, which he would seal by touching them. The part of the body he laid his hand on was thought to bear 'the Devil's Mark', and to be insensitive to pain. Witchfinders, who played an important part in many of the trials, claimed to be able to expose these tell-tale marks. They were known as 'prickers', and were paid a fee for each successful conviction.

It was obviously in the prickers' interests to prove the Devil's Mark on as many of the accused as possible, and it was common practice for some of them to use trickery or fraud to do so. The usual prickers' tool was a long, pointed needle with a handle, which was jabbed into alleged

The pricker's tool

witches after they were stripped and blindfolded. Failure to react to the pricking was interpreted as evidence of guilt, but there were various methods of cheating, including using a needle which could retract into the handle, or subtly applying some form of herbal anaesthetic to the skin.

One of the most notorious prickers was John Kincaid from Tranent in East Lothian. He was arrested and imprisoned in 1662 for wrongful torture. He was later released and, as a punishment, was banned from pricking – a sentence that would undoubtedly have been the envy of many of those he had falsely accused of witchcraft.

Execution

Some of those who were accused in a witchcraft trial managed to mount a convincing defence and were acquitted; others had the nonsensical charges against them dismissed by more enlightened courts.

But these defendants were the lucky ones. Once the charge of witchcraft had been made, the most common fate awaiting an accused was death. Most witches were burned at the stake but the majority of these were strangled first. Burning alive was the ultimate penalty for the most defiant and unrepentant witches who had tried to evade justice and shown their devotion to the Devil by refusing to confess.

In some parts of the country, the witch was made to stand in a tar barrel before burning, as this helped the flames to do their job more quickly. This was the fate of Janet Horne, the last official victim of witchcraft accusations (see p. 144).

Suicide?

Deaths in custody of those accused of witchcraft are common in the records, and it is safe to assume that many similar incidents were not considered worthy of official note.

A proportion of these deaths were certainly due to suicide. The time spent in prison, in appalling conditions, could be lengthy, and the knowledge that their imprisonment would almost certainly end in torture and a dreadful death must have driven many accused to despair. It would be surprising if the option of a swift and relatively painless suicide had not appealed to some of them.

Neglect was another cause of death in prison. The inmates were kept in unsanitary conditions, were often left in solitary confinement for months at a time, and were usually malnourished. The guards in charge of them knew that they stood little chance of reprieve, and if they became ill, little effort was made to help them. Other fatalities of the time were no doubt victims of over-zealous torture.

◆ Famous Scottish Witchcraft Trials ◆ ◆

Isobel Gowdie

One of Scotland's most notorious witches was also brought to trial in 1662. Isobel Gowdie of Auldern made a number of confessions of practising witchcraft, apparently without the usual incentive of torture.

She claimed to have made a pact with the Devil in 1647, and received various gifts and abilities from him in return. These included transforming herself into a cat, a bird or a hare; flying through the air on a straw; and being a member of a coven. She also gave details of spells, charms and Sabbat meetings, naming others in her area as fellow-members.

The significance of Isobel Gowdie's confessions is dubious. There is at least the possibility that she was mentally ill, and had created her own delusions based on the contemporary witch mythology. Whatever the explanation for her confession, there can be little doubt as to the outcome. Although contemporary sources do not record the verdict, such damning evidence would surely have resulted in executions.

Major Weir

Obsession with witchcraft spread down through society from highest to lowest, and was rife in the larger towns just as in the countryside. Another well-known case that arose in Edinburgh just a few years after Isobel Gowdie's trial illustrates how belief in witchcraft was not confined to the lower classes.

Major Thomas Weir was a well-regarded member of the Edinburgh establishment, seemingly respectable and a devout and zealous church-goer. As commander of the Edinburgh City Guards he held a responsible position within the town . He shared a house in the city's West Bow with his sister Grizel, but in the late 1660s, rumours began to circulate about the strange goings-on there.

At a prayer meeting in early 1670, Weir confirmed that the rumours were true, suddenly confessing to all manner of hideous crimes and claiming to have made a pact with the Devil, naming his sister as his accomplice. The confession was such a shock to the city's authorities that the Lord Provost sent his own doctors to check Weir's mental state. They decided that he was quite sane, suffering from no more than a guilty conscience.

The major and his sister were charged with a succession of crimes, including incest, adultery, bestiality and involvement with the Devil. Grizel also confessed, alleging that her brother's walking stick was a gift from the Devil, and was the source of their powers. After a series of sensational confessions, Major Weir and his sister were sentenced to death. Weir was burned with his stick, which was said to writhe in the flames and took as long to burn as he did. Grizel was hanged in the Grassmarket the following day.

After their executions, the Weirs' house was left empty for over a century. It was widely believed to be haunted, with unearthly shrieks, laughter and strange lights being reported in it at the dead of night. It was finally demolished in 1878.

Renfrewshire Trials

In 1692, possibly the most famous series of witch-hunts in the world took place in Salem, Massachusetts, with the prime mover behind the tragic proceedings being a young girl. But events which took place just five years later in the town of Renfrew bore an uncanny resemblance to the Salem trials.

Ten-year-old Christian Shaw had had a difference of opinion with a local woman, who was already looked on with some suspicion in the neighbourhood. Shortly afterwards, Christian fell ill, and was wracked with agonising stomach pains. Her illness reached its height when she apparently began to vomit all kinds of bizarre substances – pins, stones, eggshell and hair.

She then named the woman she claimed was tormenting her, visiting her in the form of a demon. She also went on to name around twenty others. They all stood trial and, despite the unsubstantiated nature of most of the evidence, seven were found guilty and executed by burning.

Christian Shaw's agonies stopped after the executions, and she went on to live an otherwise respectable life. She showed a great talent for spinning thread and was partly responsible for the development of the spinning industry in the Renfrewshire area.

A Hoax?

Some years after the events sparked off by Christian Shaw's illness, the room she had lain in was examined. It was found to have a secret compartment dug out of the wall, next to where her bed had been. This would have made an ideal hiding place for any of the strange materials she claimed to have vomited. The discovery effectively destroys any credibility that her testimony might have had.

Pittenweem

As the Christian Shaw case illustrates, the flimsiest of fabricated evidence could be enough to produce a guilty verdict against the hysterical background and hot-house atmosphere of Scotland's witch-hunts. But the Pittenweem trials of 1704–5 are examples of how even a verdict of not guilty did not guarantee protection from the superstitious mob.

In the Fife village of Pittenweem, a young blacksmith fell ill and blamed his sickness on a curse from a local woman, Beatrix Laing. As his illness progressed, his accusations became increasingly outrageous and he named more locals. He was very probably encouraged by the beliefs of the local minister, who visited him on his sickbed with tales of witchcraft and pacts with the Devil.

Arrested and thrown in jail, Beatrix was tortured until she named her supposed accomplices. She herself was fortunate to escape with her life: a few voices of reason on the town council were raised in her defence, protesting about the inadequate evidence, and she was released.

Her first action was to recant everything she had said in prison, which resulted in her re-arrest and imprisonment. She was soon released again with a fine, whereupon she was driven from her home by a mob of her neighbours. Although innocent, she died an outcast, never able to return to her home.

Despite Beatrix's courage in recanting, it was too late:

one of her fellow accused had already died, so neglected by the Pittenweem prison warders that he had starved. Another, Janet Cornfoot, was even less fortunate.

Janet Cornfoot

Early in 1705, the same councillors who had spoken up for Beatrix Laing came to the defence of Janet Cornfoot. They argued rightly that the accusations against her were totally unsubstantiated, and recommended her release.

Unfortunately for Janet Cornfoot, the superstitious prejudice of the locals was far stronger than the legal case against her. On 30th January 1705, she was seized by a furious mob who dragged her through the streets and beat her. She was then hauled down to the beach where heavy rocks were piled onto her chest until she was crushed to death. In one last act of injustice, the local minister then denied the innocent woman a Christian burial. No-one was ever charged in connection with her murder.

The Last Scottish Witch Trial

Twenty-two years after the murder of Janet Cornfoot, the last legal witchcraft trial in Scotland took place at Dornoch in Sutherland. Janet Horne and her daughter were both accused, the charge against Janet being that she had used her daughter as 'horse and hattock'. Under this spell, the Devil had put shoes on her hands and feet to allow her mother to ride on her back, resulting in deformities for the girl.

The daughter was released, but Janet Horne was found guilty and executed by burning in a tar barrel. Sources report how she astounded the crowd who had gathered in the winter cold to watch her die, by calmly warming her hands at the fire that was soon to consume her.

Proof of her innocence, if any were needed, came in later years when her daughter gave birth to a child with exactly the same deformity of hands and feet, obviously the result of an inherited genetic malformation.

The Casualties

The Old Testament text, 'Thou shalt not suffer a witch to live' (Exodus 12:11) took on a terrifying new significance in seventeenth-century Scotland. Contemporary records are patchy and unreliable, making an accurate assessment of the number of deaths very difficult, but some historians have put the numbers killed in the Scottish hysteria at between 3000 and 4500 overall in the century-and-a-half up to the witchcraft act's repeal in 1736.

◆ Background to the Craze ◆ ◆

The Typical Witch

The traditional picture of a witch in the popular imagination is an ugly old woman, living in isolation with only her cat for company, being hounded by the ignorant peasant mob. There were indeed many trials in Scotland where this was an accurate portrait of events: the vast majority of those found guilty were women, mostly middle-aged to elderly, and from the lower classes.

But this was no guarantee of protection for men or for those with higher social standing. It is estimated that around one in five of those accused in Scotland's witch trials were men, while the accusations ranging as far up through society as the Earl of Bothwell show that neither sex nor status was considered proof of innocence.

Women

Before the terror of the witch-hunts gripped so many areas of Scotland, women were virtually without status in the eyes of the law. Regarded as their husbands' or fathers' possessions, they were not even accepted as witnesses in Scottish courts.

As belief in the presence of witches spread, women fell under suspicion. A woman who had a history of bad temper or of wishing ill on others probably had a higher chance of being named than one who did not, and a sharp tongue directed against the wrong person could be evidence enough. The importance of reputation was shown in the accusation, with frequent references to the accused being a witch 'of ill fame', or 'by habit and repute'.

The contemporary view of women in general was that they were more inclined towards malice and sensuality, flaws of character that were compounded by their lack of reasoning. The Bible was quoted in support of this view – after all Eve, the symbol of all women, had been to blame for the fall of man in the first place.

Healers

Another factor in the trials of hundreds of women was their reputation in local communities as healers. As in most European witch trials, those who acted for the common good were vilified in the same way as those who acted for ill.

Most communities had at least one 'wise woman' who would take on various healing roles. Usually using simple herbal remedies, she would act as midwife to expectant mothers, as well as providing infusions to fight pain and infection for neighbours and even domestic animals.

Of course, in the wrong hands, such knowledge could be misused to cause illness or even death by poisoning. But the majority of these women were simply providing a much-needed service. Their problem during the witch-hunts stemmed from the fact that there was so little understanding of the scientific basis for much of this herbal medicine.

The common assumption seems to have been that, although it appeared to be beneficial, it was not understood and therefore must actually be a cover for demonic practices. Such black ignorance left many Scottish communities bereft of healers for many years.

The Devil

A firmly-held belief at all levels of Scottish society in the existence of the physical presence of the Devil was at the root of much of the country's persecution of witches.

There are few countries who have so many names for Satan – Auld Clootie, Auld Hornie, Auld Nick and the Earl of Hell are just a few. He is also found in numerous place names, including the Devil's Elbow, the Devil's Staircase and the Devil's Beeftub.

Scottish proverbs also show an awareness of demonic influence. 'He needs a lang-shankit spoon, that sups kail

The popular view of the Devil

wi' the Deil' emphasises the need for extreme caution in dealings with the Devil, while another – 'The Devil's guid to his ain' – reflects his relationship with those accused of witchcraft. The Devil could take many forms – he was a master of disguise and an accomplished shape-shifter. He also had the support of his hordes of evil minions, including fairies, goblins and kelpies.

A Witch's Pact

The pact with the Devil was the most important feature of the witch's trial – if the pricker could find evidence of the Devil's Mark, this was virtually conclusive. Many people were therefore tried and convicted on the basis of birthmarks, moles and scars.

The most significant aspect of the pact was the witch's oath of loyalty to the Devil and her promise to further his work. In return, he would ensure that she wanted for nothing. Unlike the type of satanic pact made by Dr Faustus, there was no promise of great riches: the witch was happy to think that she would be spared the desperate poverty and hunger that was the fate of many lower-class Scots. To enable the witch to carry out his work, the Devil would then bestow her with magic powers, including the ability to fly, to change herself into animal form, to influence the weather, and to cast all sorts of evil spells and charms. This was followed by feasting, music and dancing, then came the sexual debauchery that was common to virtually all witchcraft allegations. Intercourse with the Devil in some form or another was common to most Scottish trials.

Burns and the Devil

The witches' connection with the Devil is emphasised in the poet Robert Burns' *Address to the Deil*:

> Let warlocks grim, an' withered Hags,
> Tell, how wi' you, on ragweed nags,
> They skim the muirs an' dizzy crags,
>   Wi' wicked speed;
> And in the kirk-yards renew their leagues,
>   Owre howcket dead.

Another of his best-known poems, *Tam o' Shanter*, centres on the activities of witches. Making his way home on horseback after a heavy drinking session, Tam encounters a group of witches dancing at Alloway Kirk. When Tam, through an unwise display of drunken bravado, gives himself away, the witches chase him. He and Meg, his grey mare, are pursued as far as the river, reaching the bridge just as the fastest of the witches catches up with them. However, like all evil spirits, her powers are negated by running water, and she can only catch hold of Meg's tail. The brave horse gives one last surge forward, taking her rider to safety but at the cost of own her tail. (See over.)

*Tam o' Shanter and his horse, Meg,
fleeing to safety over the bridge*

◆ Reasons and Motivation ◆ ◆

No simple or single explanation has ever emerged to explain what created this apparent mass hysteria and terror of witchcraft.

Fear and ignorance seem to have been the main driving force behind this horrific period of Scottish history, supported by personal grudges, vested interests and an overheated religious hysteria. Hunting, trial and execution of witches generated a huge amount of money for the Scottish economy. Clergymen, doctors, judges, torturers,

150

executioners, prickers, prison warders and even carpenters all had a financial interest.

The Crown too had an interest in stoking the fires, both metaphorically and literally. After a conviction, all the property and goods of the witch went to the Crown, less the costs of the torture and execution which had to be paid out of their own pocket.

Geographical Variation

Some areas of Scotland saw very little of this shameful persecution. Gaelic-speaking areas of the Highlands were almost completely free of allegations. The vast majority of cases were reported in areas where the new Church was strong, including Fife, the Lothians and Aberdeenshire.

In parts of the north-east, some small villages saw multiple trials, recurring over a period of years. At the same time, parts of the north-west had none at all. It has also been suggested that communities who relied most heavily on fishing and other similarly precarious means for their livelihood were especially prone to point to witchcraft as the reason for any misfortune.

In a bizarre twist of logic, the spells of witches provided an explanation for all manner of problems and misfortunes which would otherwise have been the inexplicable work of God. Suspects in such areas were routinely accused of causing storms, sinkings, drownings and bad catches.

◆ Modern Witchcraft ◆ ◆

After the hysteria of this period had died down, witchcraft

claims and accusations became rarer in Scotland. By the twentieth century, the term 'witch' was most commonly applied as an insult to an older woman.

This did not mean the black arts were no longer practised, and in some areas, belief in the power of the supernatural continued well into the 1900s.

'The Horseman's Word'

Although its members would not have considered their practices witchcraft, the fraternity of the Horseman's Word had distinctly demonic overtones.

The cult, which supposedly gave power over horses, seems to have begun around Huntly in Aberdeenshire and was most active in the second half of the nineteenth century, continuing in some rural areas until at least the 1930s. Like almost all secret societies catering for adults, it was an exclusively male group, and initiation was regarded as a rite of passage; the means by which a boy was accepted by the local men as one of them.

Initiation ceremonies would be held in an isolated barn at midnight. The novices were blindfolded and taken there by a senior Horseman. For the ceremony, they would bare their left foot and raise their left hand, while they were told how to invoke the Devil by reading certain Bible passages backwards, and then they were given the Word itself, which would give them mastery over any horse. The ceremony ended with the blindfolded initiates shaking hands with the Devil, followed by celebratory drinking and story-telling.

The Word is still unknown to outsiders, but in 1908 a Horseman from Buchan revealed the oath taken by members. It centres around the need for secrecy, concealing the organisation and the Word from others, and obedience to the fraternity. Revealing the Word or discussing the organisation with the uninitiated would result in harsh punishment: 'If I fail to keep these promises may my flesh be torn to pieces with a wild horse and my heart cut through with a horseman's knife'.

Although the Horseman's Word was widespread, those involved kept their identity secret. Their similarities with the Freemasons are, however, glaringly obvious.

Aleister Crowley

The most notorious individual associated with modern witchcraft was Aleister Crowley, who died in 1947. Aleister Crowley claimed to be the Devil's representative on earth, and built up a considerable following. He spent a number of years in Scotland, living at Boleskin House by Loch Ness.

Not much is known about his activities while he lived at Boleskin, but strange occurrences were reported in the neighbourhood. Crowley was not strictly a witch, or even a Satanist – he explored the rituals of many pagan religions, apparently in an attempt to discover some mystical revelation. On the other hand, there are numerous tales and rumours surrounding Crowley's attempts to conjure up demons. One of these efforts ended with him temporarily confined to a mental hospital and one of his followers dead.

Crowley and his followers did adhere to certain practices of traditional witchcraft, especially those of a sexual nature. It could be that his supernatural reputation was merely a way of satisfying both a desire for notoriety and his sexual appetites.

Whatever the truth behind his time at Boleskin House, for many years visitors there have complained about a strange and sinister atmosphere.

7: Fairies

Most countries have a strong folklore relating to the supernatural beings known as 'fairies', with each place having its own idiosyncratic myths and creatures exclusive to that area.

Fairies were perceived as a very real presence in Scotland for hundreds of years and the country had a long and deep-rooted tradition of belief in a rich variety of fairies. These beings' intervention in human affairs was used to explain all sorts of odd phenomena, from incomprehensible disease and crop failure to the unexplained loss of small items and minor household breakages.

The tenacity of the Scots' belief in fairies is well demonstrated by a tale from Outer Hebrides in 1831. A labourer working on the Lewis coast came across a strangely shaped box which he broke open. Discovering dozens of small figures inside, he flung it down and fled, convinced that he had stumbled across sleeping fairies. The box actually contained eighty-four ivory chess-pieces, made by Norse craftsmen in the twelfth century and now famous in their own right as the Lewis Chessmen, in museums in Edinburgh and London.

◆ What were Fairies? ◆ ◆

Endlessly inventive speculations guessed at exactly what fairies were and at their origins, and in Scotland two explanations were particularly common.

Fairies were believed to be either fallen angels, or else the spirits of heathen dead. According to both schools of thought, they were not thought good enough to enter Heaven, but neither were they bad enough to be damned in Hell. They were therefore returned to earth in fairy form for a Purgatorial-style existence, with the form they took being a reflection of their conduct in their previous incarnation.

The idea of fairies as fallen angels is shown in references across Scotland to their dealings with the Devil. As well as helping carry out his work by tormenting mortals, they had to make a payment to him in the form of a sacrifice every seven years. This was known as the Devil's teind, from the old Lowland term for a tithe or tax. This belief is also found in parts of Ireland, and is the sinister motive occasionally given in the folklore of both countries to account for both changelings and adult kidnap by fairies.

A third theory to explain fairy origins has enjoyed some recent popularity in Scotland. It argues that belief in fairies is actually based on folk memory of the Picts, the mysterious race of indigenous people who dominated much of Scotland until the ninth century, when almost all trace of them disappeared. Some arguments could be made to support this idea – for instance, the fairies' hillside habitats could be based on the Picts' defensive ploy of concealing themselves underground to evade capture by invaders. However, it is now widely accepted that, based on study of their traditional original names, the fairy beings of Scotland can be assumed to be minor spirits associated with pagan Celtic gods.

◆ Fairy Characteristics ◆ ◆

The term 'fairies' or the Sith, as they were known in the Highlands, covers a multitude of different creatures with a variety of forms and characteristics. The traditional childhood picture of fairies as tiny, delicate, winged creatures performing good magic really only took hold in the sixteenth century, when this image became the dominant description of fairies in popular literature.

But traditionally, fairies were quite different from this pretty, benevolent picture. Many Scottish fairies, as in other parts of the British Isles, were said to be about the size of a child or a small adult. They came in many shapes, sizes and personality types, from tiny, Tinkerbell-looka-likes to huge, looming, deformed and malevolent creatures with a seemingly insatiable appetite for human blood.

But even such a diverse range of beings still shared a number of characteristics in common. Both kindly fairies and their malignant opposites possessed sensitive temperaments and took offence very easily. Like the capricious gods of Greece, it was almost impossible to predict or deduce the causes of their annoyance, as they frequently misinterpreted attempts at kindness or generosity, and took great umbrage at the most harmless actions.

This sensitivity was reflected in other ways. They were held to dislike the idea that humans knew about their existence, so it was thought best to use euphemisms to describe them. The most frequently found of these were the Good Folk, the Little People or Wee Folk, Themselves, and the Good Neighbours. Any mortal attempting deliberately to discover fairies would be severely punished if caught, and prying humans were often struck down with painful rheumatism or some other crippling condition.

Glamour

One of the main tools fairies were thought to use to hide traces of their being was the 'glamour', which concealed them from human view. This magical restriction on people's vision could be dispelled by applying fairy ointment to the eyes, allowing the person using it to see any supernatural creatures in the area. However, anyone caught using this substance without fairy permission or knowledge could expect to be blinded.

The only known exception to this harsh punishment was made for midwives, who were called on to help out at fairy births. Fairy ointment was sometimes applied to the midwife's eyes for the duration of the birth, and she was asked to apply it to the newly born fairy. If, after her return to the mortal world, a midwife with fairy ointment on her hands accidentally rubbed her eyes, she was given the benefit of the doubt, usually after a stern warning.

A four-leafed clover could also overcome the glamour, and nothing could hide fairy activity from those born with second sight, such as a seventh son of a seventh son.

Special places

Certain places, particularly woods, hills and ancient pre-Christian sites, have developed particularly close associations with fairies. One of these is Schiehallion, a peak in Perthshire. Its name is believed to derive from the Gaelic word for fairies, and is approximately translated as 'the fairy hill of the Caledonians'.

Signs of fairy activity could usually be found around these special areas, and fairy rings were a good clue. These circles of darker grass or flowers, still looked for by children today, were caused by the fairies dancing in a ring. A fairy dance ring was dangerous, as the melodic fairy music could lure unwary humans who then became caught up in the dance. They would feel that they had been dancing for a few minutes but it could be much longer – in some cases, even years – before they were allowed to leave. A well-known traditional tale in the Northern Isles tells of a young man who went through an open door into a nearby hill during a local festival, and joined the fairies dancing there. When he

A fairy hill

was rescued, he thought he had barely danced a single reel, when he had actually been trapped for a year.

This distorted perception of time was a common phenomenon for humans who communed with the fairies, like latter-day UFO abductees. This was how Thomas the Rhymer lost so much time when he became the lover of the Elf Queen.

Thomas the Rhymer

Thomas the Rhymer, whose real name was Thomas Learmont, was a real-life thirteenth-century poet and seer who lived in Erceldoune, a part of Berwickshire now known as Earlstoun.

According to the legend, Thomas was out on the charmed Eildon Hills when he fell into a reverie which seemed to him to last minutes, but in actual fact lasted for years. During this time, he was spirited away by the Queen of Elfland to become her lover. He was at last allowed to return to the mortal world, as the Devil's teind was due to be paid (see p. 156) and the queen did not want to see Thomas sacrificed. He was released on the understanding that he would return to Elfland at her summons and as he left, the fairy queen gave him the gift of prophesy, with which he was able to foretell a number of significant events in Scotland's history. These included the death of Alexander III in 1296 and the succession of Robert the Bruce to the throne; the disastrous defeat at Flodden in 1513; defeat for the supporters of Queen Mary at the 1567 Battle of Pinkie, and the Union of the Crowns in 1603. Although his prophesies were not published together until hundreds of years after his death, his writings were treated with the greatest respect.

Changelings

Although legends relate mutual benefits coming from many relationships between fairies and humans, this is was by no means always the case. One area of particular envy on the part of the fairies was human childbirth and children.

It was thought that fairies would try to steal away a newborn human baby if it was left unguarded, replacing it with a changeling – usually a sickly fairy baby. The human child suffered the fate of being brought up as a fairy and was used to provide stronger genes for future generations of fairy children.

New and nursing mothers of young babies were also at risk from the fairies, as they could be snatched and forced to nourish fairy children with their milk, which the fairies believed would give their offspring greater strength. Human midwives were also taken to help out at fairy births (see p. 158).

The Fairy Colour

Fairies are traditionally associated with the colour green, and those who wore the colour might run the risk of bringing unwelcome supernatural attention on themselves. This is the reason for the belief, which became widespread in Scotland, that green was an unlucky colour to wear. Some fairies wore green clothing or else were dressed in moss and leaves, while others still were actually green in colour.

One of these green-coloured spirits was Cu-Sith, the fairy dog of the Highlands. Fairy dogs are a common belief

Cu-Sith

throughout Britain, but in most other parts of the country they are black. Cu-Sith is described as a big dog, dark green in colour, with a shaggy coat and a long tail piled up on its back.

Protection Against The Fairies

Fairies were perceived not only as an omnipresent force in Scotland but also as a very real threat to human welfare. They routinely stirred up a fear and dread which was a commonplace of everyday life in a way that today seems difficult to imagine. As such, various precautions were devised to ward them off, or at least to weaken their influence.

Those walking alone at night would take particular care to protect themselves from any malign spirit, especially if they passed near an area known to be inhabited by fairies.

All types of fairies and spirits would be scared off by the sound of bells ringing, particularly church bells – a func-

tion traditionally performed at the end of religious ceremonies like weddings and christenings by the ringing of
the bells as the party leaves the church.

Other religious signs and symbols also had a powerful
effect. An open Bible in a baby's cradle was common protection before baptism, and reading Scripture aloud or
praying would generally see off all but the most determined spirits.

Bread was also thought to ward off fairies. It was a simple and a very common procedure for someone to place a
piece of dry bread in their pocket before they ventured out
in the evening, or passed near an area associated with
fairy activity.

Iron was thought a metal very potent against fairy interference, and was easily carried in the form of a nail or,
more usefully, a dagger or dirk. To prevent anyone suffering the fate of Thomas the Rhymer (see p. 160) and being
trapped for years inside a fairy knowe, as the hills where
they lived were known, they should take an iron dirk with
them and use it to jam open any door into the hillside.

Some plants, especially rowan and, to a lesser extent,
ash, enjoyed magical properties which, it was thought,
would also discourage fairy attentions

◆ Types of Fairies ◆ ◆

Brownies

Tales of these hard-working fairies were common all over
Scotland and in parts of north-east England. They were
usually described as looking like small men, standing at

Brownie

around two or three feet in height. They were said to have brown faces and shaggy hair, and to be dressed in the characteristic ragged brown clothes from which their name derived.

Brownies from different parts of the country were sometimes described as having distinct physical characteristics. Those in the north-east Highlands, for example, were said not to have separate fingers and toes, while some of the Lowland brownies were reputed to have no noses.

These were hard-working and benevolent beings and it was a lucky house which sheltered a brownie. Each one would attach himself to a home or farmhouse, and come out at night when the residents and servants were asleep to finish any work still left undone at the end of the day. This included looking after crops and cattle, and doing errands, cleaning and mending. Brownies were said to take a great pride in work well done: one brownie, at a house on Tiree, was even supposed to have been heard telling off the household servants for sloppiness in their own duties.

Keeping a Brownie

In common with most other Scottish fairies, the brownie was very quick to take offence. In return for his work he wanted no payment but would accept a bowl of cream or a bannock if it was left out. Puzzlingly, offering more than this might well be enough to drive a brownie away.

It may have been that the brownie was initially attracted to a home by the comforts and the food he found there, but was distrustful of anything that seemed too binding, such as being seen to accept payment. If a brownie thought too much was being offered or, conversely, if he felt unappreciated or taken for granted, he could leave the home completely, and such desertion brought bad luck on the household.

One brownie, who lived on a flourishing farm at Moffat in the Borders, took exception to an unknown slight at the hands of its owners and moved to the neighbouring Leithen Hall. There it continued to work for more than three centuries while the farm which had been its original home experienced a decline which saw it steadily sink down to ruin and bankruptcy.

Brownie to Boggart

Worse even than desertion, a previously helpful brownie might become a boggart. Boggarts were troublesome and could be very unpleasant. Their actions, contrary to those of the brownie, were designed to harass and frustrate. Minor inconveniences around the house, such as hidden or broken items, were often the work of the boggart, but he could also make bigger mischief, right up to spoiling the harvest and generally doing all he could to torment those who had offended him, no matter how unwittingly.

'Hairy Meg'

But not all brownies were male, as the legend of Meg Mullach, whose name means 'Hairy Meg', illustrates. She was a brownie who looked after the castle of Tullochgorm with her male companion, a slow-witted male brownie, and she was an excellent housekeeper.

This pair cropped up in one of the most famous tales of brownies – the story of Fincastle Mill. The mill was known to be haunted by the brownies, so it was generally avoided at night by the local people. But one evening a girl making a wedding cake for herself ran out of meal and had to go to the mill to get some more. When she was there, the male brownie appeared and asked her who she was. 'I'm Mise mi fein,' she replied, meaning 'me myself.'

To the girl's increasing alarm, the brownie continued to watch her, and she became so frightened that she eventually threw boiling water over him. He ran screaming back to Meg, and when she asked him who had been responsible, he was only able to say, 'Me myself,' before he died.

Quite some time later, after her wedding, the girl was at a ceilidh, and told the story of how she had got the better of the brownie at the mill. But her gloating proved to be her downfall: no sooner had she related the tale than a stool flew through the air and struck her on the head, killing her outright. The unseen hand of Meg Mullach had taken her revenge.

The Banshee

Like her Irish counterpart, the Scottish banshee, or Bean-Nighe as she is known in Gaelic, was believed to foreshadow death. Her name means 'washing woman', and she usually took up her stance near a river, stream or loch, where she could wash the blood-stained clothing of the unfortunate whose death she had come to foretell. She also made a wailing or crying noise, and legend claims that on the night before the massacre at Glencoe, a banshee's howl was heard all night.

Several descriptions of the banshee also testify to the fact that that she had a number of physical defects, including only one nostril and one long, protruding tooth. She also had one long, dangling breast and anyone bold enough to creep up behind her and grab it was granted a wish. However, as is so often the case in fairy encounters, the foolish human who did so usually ended up regretting it. A popular Highland ghost story tells of a man who was preparing to go into battle when he saw a banshee. He grabbed the banshee's breast and wished to know his fate. In a cryptic message, the banshee told him he would die unless his wife offered him butter without being asked. His wife did not do so, and his head was cut off during the battle. His headless spirit has haunted the battlefield ever since.

Origins of the Banshee

Some Highland legends claim that banshees are the spirits of women who have died in childbirth, who were obliged to perform their ritual of warning others of their impending demise until the day when they themselves should have died.

Cailleach Bheur

Sometimes mistaken for a banshee, Cailleach Bheur was actually a terrifyingly described blue-faced hag whose home was in the Highlands. She also crops up under different names but in similar legends in other parts of the country. In northern parts of Ireland she is known as Cally Berry, and she is Caillagh ny Gromagh in the Isle of Man.

She is almost certainly a product of the primitive beliefs of the ancient Celts, and is the mythological remnant of their goddess of winter. Throughout the winter she was believed to curse the earth to kill the growth, and could conjure up fearful storms, winds and blizzards. On Beltane Eve, she turns into a block of stone, and remains in that state until her rebirth with the onset of winter on Hallows' Eve.

Trows

The influence of Scandinavian culture on Scotland's northern islands is illustrated by the legends of the trows. They are undoubtedly Shetland's version of the Scandinavian trolls, with the same physical description – that of ugly little dwarfs – as they had in their homeland, and the same sullen and unpleasant nature. They dressed in grey, and were often known by the euphemistic name, 'the Grey Neighbours'. Trows lived underground, were well known for their dislike of daylight and, like most fairies, were fiercely possessive about their habitat.

According to one legend, the trows of Orkney felt so threatened by the coming of civilisation to the main islands that they tried to walk across a tightrope strung across to the quieter nearby island of Hoy. The plan went badly wrong, however: the tightrope snapped, and the Orkney trows were drowned.

However, another story, told as late as the early twentieth century, suggested that all the trows may not have drowned on the trip to Hoy. It related how an Orkney trow warned a local farmer not to dig up a mound on his land, threatening that this would result in the farmer losing six cows, which would be followed by six funerals. The man persisted, and very shortly lost not only the cattle but also six members of his family.

Some sightings of trows reported them 'henking' – this was a particular dance performed by the trows, who were slightly lame. This gave rise to their other name, 'Henkies.' Henking involved squatting down on the ground with their hands clasped around their thighs, then leaping up and kicking out alternate legs. Although this particular dance is associated only with trows, almost all fairies were said to have loved to dance.

Redcap

Redcaps

But there were other, far more malevolent fairies, some of whom were among the most terrifying creatures in Scottish mythology. The redcap was one of these – an evil goblin who haunted ruined towers and castles where particularly wicked deeds had taken place.

Centuries ago, the wicked lord of Hermitage Castle supposedly had a redcap to assist him in his tyranny, and his supernatural partner helped him to remain invincible by normal weapons. He was eventually killed only after being boiled in a cauldron of oil.

Redcap's forbidding name came from his gruesome habit of dyeing his cap in human blood. He was very powerful and could not be overcome by any normal human means. Instead, the only effective means to repel him was, vampire-like, with the sign of the cross or a Bible.

◆ Water Spirits ◆ ◆

Scotland's particular physical characteristics, with its many lochs, rivers and waterfalls, have also given rise to their own legends, based around sea-creatures. Just like the spirits that are exclusively land-based, the water fairies are a mixture of good and bad.

Selkies

Selkies could take the form of seals or humans, depending on whether they were in the water or on land. Said by some to be a Scottish version of the mermaid myth, they took human form when they removed their seal skins. The name selkies, or silkies, probably derives from the silky texture of seal skin. By all accounts a very gentle race, they seem to have been most commonly reported around the northern and western islands.

Selkie Relations with Humans

Once their seal-skins were removed, selkies became

extremely attractive to humans, and it was common for people who came into contact with them to fall in love. Occasionally the feeling was mutual and the selkie would make the decision to stay on land. Male selkies seem to have been fairly amorous, and would form occasional liaisons with mortal women, but most cases of a selkie and human match were forced.

Selkie

Men would steal the seal-skins of the selkie women and hide them. This meant the selkie was trapped and she would have to agree to stay with a man and become his wife. Any children produced by such a selkie–human union would have webbed hands and feet. No matter how long she lived with her mortal husband and the family ties she built up, the selkie would always pine to return to the sea.

One particular legend from Shetland tells of a selkie woman who had been married to her mortal husband for many years and had a number of children with him. One day their son came across her seal skin hidden away in his father's hiding place. He took it to his mother and asked her what it was. His delighted mother instantly seized the skin, put it on and slipped into the water, evading by seconds the grasp of her returning spouse to leave him, their children and their home behind forever.

Kelpies

Kelpies, and their Highland equivalent Each Uisge, were among the most malevolent and dangerous of the supernatural creatures to be found in Scottish mythology. The kelpie is the best known of the two types of water-horse – it was usually found by running water, while the Each Uisge preferred seas and lochs. Malevolent water spirits like kelpies were known to lure travellers into deep water at what looked like shallow, crossable waters, so fords and crossing points were thought particularly dangerous places.

The creature also carried unsuspecting travellers into deep waters on its back. In these circumstances it would appear in the form of a young horse, apparently very docile, then parade itself in front of unsuspecting victims, seemingly inviting them to get on its back. With its prey on board, the kelpie would then bolt into the water, its victim magically unable to dismount, dragging the rider down with it to be drowned or, in the case of the Each Uisge, devoured, with only their liver left floating on the water.

A typical tale of a fairy water-horse comes from the Aberfeldy area. Eight local children were playing on the shores of nearby Loch Tay when they saw a young pony. It seemed very tame and friendly and, one after another, the children climbed up onto its back.

The last child due to mount, a boy, was more cautious, seeing something strange about a pony whose back seemed to grow longer to accommodate the number of children sitting on it. He moved back to hide among the shoreside rocks, and watched as the now-revealed kelpie dashed headlong into the water. The seven screaming and terrified children were unable to get off its back, and all were drowned in the loch.

Working a Kelpie

There was one way a kelpie could be controlled, and that was if someone managed to sneak up and put a human bridle on it. It could then be ridden without danger, but only while it was wearing the bridle.

However, forcing a kelpie to work and wear a bridle

could be a risky business, as one particular laird discovered. Graham of Morphie, near Montrose, managed to harness one on the River North Esk which ran by his lands. He hooked the water-horse up to a cart and drove it repeatedly backwards and forwards, carrying stones to build his new castle. When the work was finished, the exhausted kelpie was released, only to swear a curse on Graham, that his family would never flourish while they lived at the new house at North Esk. Of course, the line eventually failed, and the estate passed on to another family.

Shetland's Noggle

Also known as the 'nygel', this is the version of the kelpie that is found in the Shetland Isles. This was a creature smaller and less malevolent than the others. Mostly found around mills, it usually preferred to give its victims a good ducking rather than kill them.

Blue Men of the Minch

As their name suggests, the malevolent Blue Men were found only in the Minch, specifically the strait between Lewis and the Shiant ('Charmed') Islands. The name of this stretch of water, 'Sruth nam fear Gorm', means 'the Sound of the Blue Men', and they were traditionally held to be responsible for its treacherous weather.

These beings are usually described, not surprisingly, as being blue in colour, around human size, and with long grey beards. They appeared to ships in the strait, waving their long arms above the water to lure their victims, siren-like, to the choppiest waves.

Riddles of the Blue Men

Once the Blue Men had their sights set on a vessel, they were unshakeable in their pursuit. But a quick-witted captain might still be able to escape their clutches.

Before they attempted to sink a ship, the Blue Men had a habit of posing its captain a cryptic riddle. If the captain could answer correctly, he and his ship were allowed to pass unharmed. But one wrong answer would see the vessel wrecked and all aboard dragged down to their deaths in the Blue Men's deep underwater caves.

Possible Origins

While popular Highland tradition claimed the Blue Men were fallen angels, their legend may actually have had a recognisable historical origin.

The northernmost islands of Scotland were under Scandinavian control for several hundred years. In the ninth century, during this period of Viking rule, these Norse warriors are known to have taken captives from North African boats. Their Moorish prisoners were taken on to Ireland, a route which may have brought them through Scottish waters. The Moors are believed to have had long beards and to have worn their traditional dress, blue veils and clothes – in all, bearing more than a passing similarity to the seemingly fanciful descriptions of the Blue Men.

Nuckelavee

This Orcadian sea creature seems to have been among the most blood-thirsty and hideous of its kind. It had the upper body of a man, coming out of the lower body of a huge horse, like a centaur. Its arms were very long, reaching almost to the ground, and most gruesome of all, it had no skin.

Nuckelavee would rise out of the water, killing any people or animals unfortunate enough to cross its path, and destroying crops. The only possibility of escape was to cross a running stream or river – as a sea spirit, Nuckelavee did not like fresh water.

◆ The Seelie and Unseelie Courts ◆ ◆

The collective term in Scottish mythology for the benevolent fairies was the Seelie Court. They generally behaved kindly towards the humans they came into contact with, providing them with assistance and showing immense gratitude for the slightest kindness.

The other types of Scottish fairies were to be found in the Unseelie Court. This was made up of all the malicious fairies who set out only to do harm and destroy. The host included such horrors as Redcap and Nuckelavee, and they harboured only the most evil intentions.

The Seelie Court were generally thought to take to the skies around twilight, while the Unseelie Court preferred to fly in the dead of night, picking up any unfortunate or foolhardy mortals who happen to venture out unprotected into their path. They dragged their victims along, beat them and forced them to take part in their malicious work, which usually involved the harassment of and cruelty towards other humans and animals. Part of this work included the scattering of elf-shot, the mysterious fairy substance that would render insensible those unlucky enough to be struck by it. Any inexplicable illness in humans or animals would be attributed to elf-shot. An illustration of the power it was credited with is illustrated in the modern medical term 'stroke', which comes directly from 'elf-struck', the description applied to the victims of elf-shot.

◆ The Fairy Flag of Dunvegan ◆ ◆

Scotland's most famous fairy legend, and one which is said to have a tangible link to the fairies themselves, involved a gift to the MacLeod family of Dunvegan on

Skye – the Fairy Flag. This magical flag, also known in Gaelic as Bratach Sith, is legendary among the MacLeod clan, and supposedly safeguards them against their enemies. Surprisingly mundane and unspectacular in appearance – a mustard yellow or brown square, with patches of red darning – it is kept at the seat of the clan, Dunvegan Castle on Skye.

Centuries ago the MacLeod chief fell in love with a fairy. The pair married and had a son, but after the birth her people called her back and she was obliged to go. She left the child with his father, and they parted at the spot known as the Fairy Bridge, near Dunvegan.

The father arranged for a nursemaid to look after the child. One night not long after the mother's departure, the clan had gathered for a get-together which ended with a ceilidh. The careless nursemaid left the baby alone, intending to go and join in the fun, and in her absence the child kicked off his covers, then began to cry with the cold. The noise of her son's crying reached his supernatural mother who sneaked back into the castle unseen, covered him with a square of silk and sang to him until he was asleep.

The nursemaid returned from the ceilidh in time to hear the fairy song, but she could not see the baby's mother. She picked up the child and took him and the silk square to his father, the chief, telling of what she had found and the song she had heard in the seemingly empty nursery. This piece of silk left by the fairy is the MacLeods' fairy flag, while the song the fairy mother sang to her child is still occasionally heard in Skye, and is known as the *Dunvegan Lullaby*.

Legend of the Flag

The legend which grew up around the flag stated that, if the clan was in danger, unfurling the flag would save them by summoning for them supernatural assistance. But like all the best magic, it carried limitations and drawbacks: it could only be used three times, and a terrible punishment would befall Skye if the flag were flown for a trivial reason.

To date, the flag has been used twice. Both times were in the Middle Ages and against the MacLeods' enemies the MacDonalds. Despite being hopelessly outnumbered on each occasion, after waving the flag, the MacLeods were victorious. As a good-luck charm, family and clan members even carried photographs of the flag into battle with them in the Second World War.

Other Possible Origins

There are other legends claiming to explain the origins of the flag. Some experts who have examined it claimed its fibres and design indicate that it came from Syria or possibly Rhodes, suggestions which gave rise to the theory that it had been brought back from the Crusades at some point in the MacLeod history.

Another romantic legend is that it was actually the flag used by the defeated Harald Hardrada at the Battle of Stamford Bridge in 1066. Although he was a Norseman, Harald had previously also fought in the east with the Byzantine army, a history which would go a long way to explaining the eastern origins of the flag. And given the very close connection that existed between Scandinavia and the Scottish islands until the thirteenth century, the cloth could well have changed hands from Norse to Scottish ownership.

8: Monsters

Scotland's location as a dark, dank outpost on the north-westernmost fringes of Europe have ensured a rich tapestry of folk tales and legends of lurking monsters. The earliest recorded sighting of a monster dates from the seventh century, and presents a description which remains familiar at fourteen centuries' remove. In fact, quite a few of Scotland's monster legends have proved potent and enduring enough to last down to the present day.

◆ The Millennium Factor ◆ ◆

The arrival of the new millennium will certainly ensure that notions of the unexplained and the paranormal are kept to the forefront of many minds, and monster legends in particular seem to excite contemporary interest in a way that stories of fairies do not.

Although they may seem to overlap, legends of monsters are quite distinct from those of fairies. For one thing, they rarely have the same supernatural connotations: according to the stories, monsters were often destructive and malicious, but not demonic. They are unexplained but definitely earthly, rather than necessarily un- or supernatural. It is even possible that these monster legends were based on real creatures. Like Chinese whispers, the versions of such monster stories now current may not be as they were first told generations ago, but it is always possible that, for example, tales of dragons could be based on large lizards or snakes.

Another factor that separates fairy and monster legends is that of credibility. While it is extremely rare in modern times for anyone to believe in fairies, many otherwise sceptical adults are reluctant to dismiss the idea of these legendary monsters.

It may be that a belief in kelpies, brownies and their like seems just too far-fetched to modern, more scientifically aware minds. But the idea of a monster that is some kind of prehistoric throwback, or a dragon legend based on a giant squid, has some, albeit tenuous, basis in scientific or biological fact for a phenomenon otherwise fantastical.

◆ *Types of Monsters* ◆ ◆

Dragons and 'Worms'

In general terms, the word 'dragon', originally of Greek origin, derived from the term for a large snake and was used to describe any creature that appeared to be basically reptilian. Legends of dragons are common throughout the British Isles, although each area has added its own twist to the traditions. Over seventy villages or small towns have their own local dragon legend.

physical Characteristics

All the creatures that fell under the heading of 'dragon' tended to have other things in common besides their snake-like appearance. If their bodies were cut or parts were severed, they would join up again, just as in the popular childhood myth about worms. They also shared similar character traits. While legends in the Far East and China describe dragons as benevolent beings with a strong moral code, this was certainly not the case in Britain. In general, the home-grown variety were thought to be destructive and cruel; ferocious and greedy creatures who would attack without provocation.

Scotland's dragon-like creatures were traditionally described as 'worms', although this should not be taken to mean that their physical stature was less impressive than a dragon.

Unlike other dragons throughout the world, and indeed many parts of Britain, these Scottish worms did not have wings. There are no reports of flying dragons, and very few of the dragon legends even mention their having legs. Their method of moving was more like that of a snake or a worm, too. They would crawl along the ground on their bellies, so judging by this description, the term 'worm' is a more accurate one.

They would coil their bodies around things – the hills where they often lived, or the unfortunate people or cattle that were their prey. The worms had foul, poisonous breath that they would also use to stun or kill their victims; in fact, their breath was sometimes described as being fiery – a description reminiscent of the traditional notion of a dragon.

The Linton Worm

The legendary twelfth century Linton Worm is the most famous of the Scottish dragons. It was a huge snake-like creature, at least twelve feet long, and lived in a tunnel on Linton Hill in Roxburghshire, close to the border with England. It emerged twice a day, at dusk and dawn, to feed on anything it could find, including local people, crops and animals, terrorising as it did a large area of the Borders around the village itself and as far away as the town of Jedburgh. It seemed indestructible. Numerous men from the area had found out to their cost that traditional weapons like spears and arrows were useless against it.

The Linton Worm

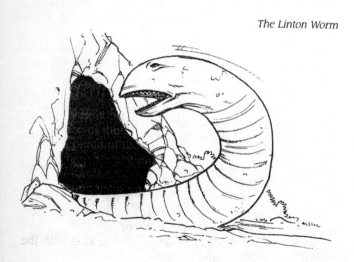

A local Scots–Norman laird, John de Somerville, decided he would have to be the one to kill it. He spent some time reconnoitring, watching the worm to see if he could spot any clues as to how to fight it. He realised that it could not move backwards, but had to move in a circle to get back to its den. He also noticed that whenever it encountered anything too big to fit into its mouth, it would stop with its mouth open, as though it was trying to work out how to fit it in.

Somerville had constructed a special spear that was twice as long as normal and coated in iron to protect it from the worm's venomous, melting breath. He attached a special holder to the end of it, which contained a ball of peat soaked in pitch.

Just before dawn, when the worm was due to emerge, Somerville rode up on his horse to the creature's cave, watched by the locals. As the worm came out, he rode towards it and it stopped as he had anticipated, mouth open at the sight of the man and horse which together were too big for it to swallow. Somerville lit the peat and thrust it right into the beast's throat. The worm could not back away, allowing Somerville to lodge it firmly in its entrails before making his escape.

Writhing in agony, the worm whipped its tail in a coil around a hill, squeezing it and creating ridges. Flickings of the tail as it writhed were also said to have created the undulations on the hills around the area that came to be known as Wormington, where it supposedly lived. The worm finally brought the roof of its tunnel down on itself, and it perished under a huge shower of earth.

John de Somerville was rewarded by the king with the post of royal falconer and the lands and barony of Linton, and his bravery and ingenuity was commemorated on a specially-carved stone at Linton Kirk.

Other Worms

In other areas where such ridges are found in the landscape, similar explanations are found. Cnoc-na-Cnoimh in Sutherland was the scene of another epic battle in the late twelfth century like that won by John de Somerville at the other end of the country. The legend here is illustrated even in the area's name, which is Gaelic for 'Worm's Hill'. It has the characteristic ridges supposedly caused by the dying worm, which was again cleverly killed with only a burning peat as a weapon. The hero on this occasion was a local farmer, Hector Gunn, who was rewarded with land and money by King William I, the Lion.

Similar stories can also be found in Argyll and Kirkton of Strathmartine in Angus. Another centres around Dalry, where a huge white worm was coiled around Mote Hill, wreaking havoc in the neighbourhood. It was killed in dramatic fashion by a local blacksmith, who supposedly made himself a special dragon-proof suit. This was a suit of armour covered with retractable spikes. With the spikes covered, he allowed the dragon to swallow him, but once he was inside he pushed the spikes out and began to roll around, killing the monster from the inside.

◆ Sea Monsters ◆ ◆

All island countries have some tradition of sea monsters, and Scotland has been no exception to this. Considering that the country is surrounded by water on three sides and has numerous islands, it is perhaps surprising that there are not more legends of sea monsters. There are some reports of Highland sea monsters, including one known as Mial mhor a chuain, which is Gaelic for 'the great beast of the ocean.'

Mester Stoorworm

> 'His breath was so venomous that when he
> was angry and blew out a great blast of it,
> every living thing within reach was destroyed
> and all the crops were withered."

'Muckle Mester Stoorworm', the sea monster which inspired this vivid description, is one of the most dramatic monster legends to appear in Scotland's folklore. The tale originates in Orkney where the beast supposedly came to live in the waters around the island.

The creature was said to be so enormous that it could wrap its body right around the earth. It demanded to be fed seven virgins every week to satisfy its hunger and placate its fierce temper, a situation which, hardly surprisingly, the local people soon decided could not continue.

The king's adviser said the only other option was to offer the monster the king's own daughter, the astonishingly named Princess Gemdelovely, in the hope that such a huge sacrifice would persuade it to go elsewhere. The king, evidently a less than fond father, found himself agreeing on grounds which were decidedly unusual for a monarch – that he could not possibly ask his subjects to do more than he himself was prepared to do to get rid of the beast. However, he first appealed for a champion to come forward and kill the creature, with the reward not only of the princess's hand in marriage, but of the kingdom itself.

While in some ways the legend of Mester Stoorworm is like a fairytale, it has some significant departures from this tradition. One is the social status of the hero: while princes and other noblemen appear in the story to confront the huge worm, they either die in the attempt or else are so terrified by the sight of the monster that they simply run away. The unlikely hero who determines to fight the beast and win is Assipattle, a local lad who was something akin to a David figure. He was a charmed seventh son, the youngest brother who although he was highly imaginative, was also immensely lazy.

When the king called for a champion to save his daughter, Assipattle decided to act. Like John de Somerville with the Linton Worm, Assipattle watched the monster's behaviour for a few days, noting its habits and plotting his campaign. One morning, he put his plans into action: sneaking away from home on his father's magic horse and carrying with him a ball of peat, he stole the king's boat, rowed out to where the monster was, and waited for it to yawn, as he knew from his observations that it would. When it did so, he and his boat were sucked inside with the water it swallowed.

Once inside the monster's intestines, Assipattle lit the ball of peat he had brought, then embedded it into the creature's liver. He was safely expelled from Mester Stoorworm's flaming intestines when the creature began roaring and retching in agony from the pain.

After its death, the huge body of the worm was said to have formed the island of Iceland, while the teeth which it spat out in its dying torments were to become the Orkney and Shetland islands.

In the best fairytale tradition, Assipattle and the Princess Gemdelovely were married, and lived happily ever after as fair and just rulers, with many children and grandchildren.

◆ Loch Monsters ◆ ◆

With such a rich history in all sorts of folklore, Scotland's mythological culture also extends to creatures living in the country's many lochs. These are more popular and certainly more widely known than the legends of sea monsters.

In terms of their appearances, these loch monsters superficially seem to bear a resemblance to the water-dwelling dragons such as Mester Stoorworm. They are usually described as looking snake-like, with long necks. Temperamentally, though, they seem very different. The loch-dwellers seem to avoid human contact, and reports of them being aggressive, particularly in unprovoked incidents, are rare. This is possibly the reason why the loch monsters are so rarely the subject of slaying legends.

Unlike many of their monstrous contemporaries, the legends of some of these Scottish loch creatures persist to the present day. They are not just related in Scotland, but are known throughout the world.

The most famous of Scotland's water monsters is said to reside, of course, in Loch Ness, but Nessie has other, less famous siblings. In the past, Gaelic names were given to the three most famous: An Niseag, in Loch Ness, A'Mhorag, who lived in Loch Morar, and An Seileag in Loch Shiel. Of course there were others, not so well known or well documented, but it is of Nessie and, to a lesser extent, Morag, that most has been seen and written.

The Loch Ness Monster

Despite numerous explorations using the most sophisticated technology, Loch Ness is still a mysterious place. Around 24 miles long and one mile wide, it is extremely deep. The average depth is about 700 feet but there are thought to be many deeper areas.

Such an unexplored territory makes an ideal backdrop for one of the most enduring Scottish legends, and one of the most well-known, The story of the Loch Ness Monster has become known around the globe and the nickname it has acquired, Nessie, is a sign of the affection with which it is regarded.

The First Sighting: St Columba

It was to the monk Adamnan, the seventh-century biographer of St Columba, that the fame fell of being the first to record a sighting of an *aquatilis bestia* at Loch Ness – the Loch Ness Monster or, more probably, its ancient ancestor. Adamnan, obviously well aware that his credibility would be at stake, insisted in his commentary on the episode that he was recording something that had actually happened.

On their travels through the north, Columba and his followers were required to cross the River Ness which connects the loch to the Moray Firth. At the shore they came across a burial party for a man who had, the mourners insisted, recently been the victim of the monster in the loch. But Columba still wanted to cross, and ordered one of his monks, Lugne Mocumin, to swim to the far bank and bring back a boat which was tied there.

Lugne was half-way across the chilly river when the monster suddenly surfaced near him and turned, bearing down on the now-terrified monk. Columba, unflinching, rebuked the roaring beast, loudly instructing it to turn back while making the sign of the cross. The monster drew up short, sank back beneath the water and swam away.

Modern Investigation

Adamnan's proved to be the first written account in what has now become a long line of apparent sightings of something in the cold, deep waters of the loch. It is also the only one to record the monster behaving in such a threatening way; in other sightings, the monster usually seems oblivious to or unconcerned by the human presence. Some subsequent reports spoke of seeing shapes like an upturned boat moving at speed through the water; others reported seeing shapes like a serpent or giant eel in the water, with a giant body tapering to a small, narrow head.

The number of sightings increased greatly since the lochside road opened the area up to easy visitor access in the 1930s. In all, there have been thousands of sightings in the years since Adamnan's, and many times that number of visitors to the loch, ranging from tourists passing through, to film crews and scientists determinedly staying for weeks. Most have left disappointed.

Modern Theories

Over the many years of suspicion of a presence in the loch, a number of theories have been put forward by way of explanation.

One of these is that the monster is in fact some kind of prehistoric survivor – possibly a plesiosaur – and that, given the different sizes reported in various sightings, there may even be a family of dinosaur-type creatures living in the loch. This may not be as far-fetched as it first seems, as creatures previously thought to have been extinct for millions of years have occasionally been discovered, very much alive. The theory goes that the monsters, by sheltering in the dark, near 1000-foot-deep loch waters, were able to survive the devastating upheaval of the Ice Age on Scotland's climate and topography, and have lived on, albeit in some evolved and modified form, to the present day.

Cameras and videos have claimed to record the movements of the monster, but in recent years even more advanced technology has been used. Sonar and radar scans have proved inconclusive. The loch's murky waters are filled with vague shapes and shadows that could be anything from a shoal of fish through strange wave formations to a drifting shopping trolley. But there is still the tantalising possibility that it could be something else.

Undoubtedly, people like the idea of the Loch Ness Monster – and not just locals who benefit from the tourism generated by the legend. The romantic idea of a creature living on under such circumstances and so much against the odds, has huge appeal. But if anything is lurking in the loch depths it seems content to stay there, and most Scots are probably glad that conclusive proof of Nessie's non-existence will, in all likelihood, never be found – the country's cultural heritage would certainly be much the poorer.

Loch Morar

The monster reported to be resident in Loch Morar, which rejoices in the name of Morag, is less well known than her sister in Loch Ness, probably because Morar is in a more inaccessible part of Inverness-shire, and because she has been seen less often.

Vague stories had been around for a few hundred years that the loch might be home to something more than fish. But it was only in 1969 that the attention of Scotland's monster hunters was brought firmly to Morar, for a change. Two local fishermen were sailing their small boat down the loch when it was almost capsized by what they described as a large brown creature, around 25 feet long, with a snake-like head and an undulating, humpy back. They had tried to fend off the beast with an oar, and continued to watch it for the next five minutes until it swam out of their sight. The following year the Loch Morar Survey was set up, recording past sightings and conducting experiments, but nothing conclusive was found. It could be that this stunningly beautiful stretch of water on the single-track road to Mallaig was spared intensive, Loch Ness-style investigation by its remoteness.

One explanation that has been suggested for the similarity in the descriptions of the monsters in the two lochs is that Morag and Nessie are one and the same. An underground and as yet unknown passage linking the two deep lochs would make it easy for the same monster to swim between one and the other.

◆ Other Phenomena ◆ ◆

Few of Scotland's legends and myths can trace their possible origins back as far as the Loch Ness Monster, over a period of fourteen hundred years. But myths do not have to be old to be sinister or bizarre: one of the most elusive and frightening myths has only emerged in the last hundred years or so.

The Big Grey Man

Ben MacDhui is the highest mountain in the Cairngorms at 4296 feet, and the second-highest peak in Scotland after Ben Nevis. Stories of the mountain's Big Grey Man (in Gaelic, Am Fear Liath Mór or Am Fear Glas Mór) have circulated for over a century, making him one of the most recent legends of his type in Scottish mythology.

First Sighting

The first person to report experiencing a malevolent presence of the Grey Man was Norman Collie from Aberdeenshire. He had all the credentials of a credible witness in the situation: as well as being an experienced climber, he was also a professor of chemistry at the University of London – not a man for whom hysteria or an over-ripe imagination was usual.

He reported in 1925 that on a solitary climb on Ben MacDhui in 1891, thirty-four years previously, he had felt aware of another presence walking down the mountain just behind him. Although there was no other climber near him, the sound of the footsteps was very clear, keeping time with his. But eerily, he estimated from the sound that the walker was taking steps three or four times the length of his own. A sinister impression of being shadowed by a huge and menacing creature grew upon him, and he ran, careering down the slope as fast as he could until he was safe at the mountain foot. He never went on the mountain alone again.

Since then, a number of other climbers have told of similar experiences. Most of the reports share certain common features: the climbers were usually on their own when they became aware of a shadowy figure that filled them with terror and, as they fled, pursued them for long distances down the slope. One terrified climber claimed to have been pursued as far as the outskirts of Braemar, some eleven miles from the mountain. Some have reported being drawn as if magnetically to the edge of dangerous ledges and precipices; others, less fortunate, have been believed to have been chased to their deaths, in their terror to escape, over the edge of the cliff known as Lurcher's Crag.

Physical Characteristics

Of those who claim to have seen the Grey Man, rather than just felt his presence, descriptions of his appearance is fairly vague. There are some common factors – he is very tall, around eight or ten feet, with very long arms and legs. He is also described as being covered in hair, and a couple of reports claimed that he was wearing a 'lum' hat, or top hat.

Theories of the Grey Man

With the exception of the hat, descriptions of the Grey Man sound similar to descriptions of the North American Sasquatch, and to the Yeti in the Himalayas. Some scientists do accept that sightings of these creatures seem to have some basis in fact. Other, less detached observers have wondered if the Big Grey Man in the Cairngorms might be a similar type of being to his other mountain counterparts.

An obvious explanation is that the alleged sightings are nothing but hallucinations brought on by exhaustion, isolation or altitude. Yet most of the sightings have been reported by experienced climbers who have dealt with similar conditions on other peaks without experiencing any untoward sensations or hallucinations. Sceptics have also explained him away as a product of the misty weather conditions of the Cairngorm plateau, yet sightings have been reported in all types of conditions, from sunny summer days to winter blizzards.

'Spectre of the Brocken'

This is a phenomenon which has been reported by climbers all over the world. The shadow of the person is thrown against an opaque wall of mist by a low sun, causing a magnified and distorted image to appear to them. Such an experience has been reported by many on the Scottish mountains, including the writer James Hogg, known as the Ettrick Shepherd, in the 1790s.

Such a sight, coupled with the other factors of isolation, snow and altitude, could perhaps provide the explanation to the myth of the Grey Man. But even if it explained the legend and the shadowy sightings, it would not account for the physical evidence that has supposedly been found. Huge footprints, not made by humans or animals, have been found and photographed in the snow on Ben MacDhui. In 1965, prints were discovered that were around fourteen inches long, with a stride that would have covered around five feet – not unlike Professor Norman Collie's guesstimate during his panicky descent down the mountainside in 1891.

Arguments about the creature's existence still go on, despite the fact that it has been some years since the last reported sighting. The Big Grey Man of Ben MacDhui continues to be an elusive and unexplained legend of the Highlands.

9: Saints

◆ Scotland's Religion ◆ ◆

Religion and its diverse influences has, until relatively recently, played an important part in Scots
life and society, both before and after the divide
that was the religious Reformation of the sixteenth century. Pre- and post-Reformation opinions pulled the country
this way and that, from debates over how church services
should be conducted to how Christmas should be celebrated (see ch. 4).

But the rules of Church and society always ran in parallel, especially after 1560, when the new Church of
Scotland's forbidding-sounding 'godly discipline' was
imposed on the country at large. Stern and enthusiastic
reformers, finding themselves with free reign in the relative power vacuum of the time, were almost frenzied in
their despatching of much that was familiar in the religious landscape.

But it says much for the enduring and powerful mythology of Scotland's saints that, while churches and monasteries were shattered by reformers who eschewed any

belief in either canonisation or sainthood, the saints who bore their names continued to be revered and respected by the ordinary people. In fact the nation's saints, with their attendant cults and customs, were one of the few enduring symbols of Scotland's religion down through the centuries.

St Andrew

Nationally and internationally, the foremost among Scotland's saints is the country's patron, St Andrew.

A fisherman on the Sea of Galilee, Andrew was one of the first disciples to follow Jesus. He was the brother of Simon Peter and was among the first four apostles mentioned in the Gospels. After Jesus' death Andrew began evangelising, spreading Christianity through the eastern Mediterranean region, before being martyred at Patras in Greece around 60 AD.

The Scottish Connection

The association of St Andrew with Scotland arose centuries after his death. One legend stated that the monk who was to become St Rule set off for Scotland after an angel appeared to him in a dream and told him to take Andrew's remains there. His remains were then carried from Patras by Rule to 'a region towards the west, situated in the utmost part of the world'. He finally came ashore at Kinrymont in Fife, after his vessel was shipwrecked. Another version stated that Rule came to Scotland only by accident.

Whatever the reason for his visit to Scotland, once there Rule brought ashore the holy relics, believed to be an arm bone, a knee cap, a tooth and three fingers. Such remains were precious and highly desirable items in the medieval world, particularly from such a high profile star in the saintly firmament as Andrew.

Rule began building a church in the spot where the bones were laid to rest, which was already a site of worship of the Celtic Church and may even have dated from pre-Christian times. The settlement he founded became known as St Andrews and became a major shrine, with pilgrims including St Margaret among its visitors. Rule himself was the first bishop of St Andrews in the eighth century.

After his death the cult of St Andrew developed quickly. His feast was celebrated from the sixth century on, and churches were dedicated to him in Italy, France and Anglo-Saxon England. Around the time of the first millenium in 1000, Andrew was adopted as Scotland's national patron saint and his feast day – also celebrated in Russia, of which he is patron – is 30th November. It is an evening of celebration for Scots at home and abroad, and while the day is still observed in celebratory Masses and other church services, most festivities these days have very little to do with religion.

The Saltire or St Andrew's Cross

According to some legends, Andrew's executioners were set to crucify him in the conventional upright style, but he protested that he was not worthy to die in the same way as Jesus. He supposedly persuaded them to change the shape of the cross, and so the X-shape, known as the saltire, was used instead. This is the shape which appears on the Scottish flag, and on official emblems and badges

The bedge of the Royal Scots

of various organisations, such as the Royal Scots Regiment.

The traditional story to explain the Scots' adoption of the flag dates back to the eighth century. The Pictish king Hungus, faced with an advancing Northumbrian army, had a dream where St Andrew appeared and promised him victory. When the king awoke, he saw a cross-shaped cloud formation in the night sky, which inspired him to lead his forces to victory at Aethelstaneford.

Around the year 1000, at the time Andrew was adopted as the country's patron saint, the saltire began to appear as a symbol of Scotland. From the mid-fourteenth century, it was used on coins and had started to feature on flags by the 1500s. After 1707 the Union Flag, incorporating the saltire, was adopted as the single flag of Britain, but the saltire remained popular in Scotland. It is still recognised as the national flag of Scotland, and is flown outside many of the country's public buildings.

Although the X-shaped cross is central to the legend of Andrew, the story is open to doubt. In depictions of his crucifixion, the saltire does not appear until the Middle Ages; earlier representations show a traditional cross.

St Ninian

St Ninian, or Nynia, is the first named Christian saint of Scottish record, and is strongly associated with the country. Although he first brought Christianity to Scotland, his activities are less well chronicled than those of other saints and missionaries, such as Columba.

Ninian's own origins are unknown: different sources claim he was either from the south-west, possibly around Galloway, or from Wales; he may even have been the son of a converted British chieftain. He trained in Rome, from where he may have been sent to establish his own see in Scotland at the start of the fifth century. He preached among the pagans in the southern half of Scotland, and some historians claim he may also have worked in Fife and Angus, helping to convert other areas which were later to lapse.

Whithorn

Such was Ninian's success that his base at Whithorn in Wigtownshire, where he was eventually buried, became known as the cradle of Christianity in Scotland, and remained for centuries one of the country's foremost centres of pilgrimage. Crowds flocked from all over the country right up to the Reformation, with many royal visitors among them. These included Robert I (the Bruce) and James IV, a frequent visitor, praying for atonement for his part in the death of his father, and one time even making the trip on foot to pray for the health of his wife, Margaret Tudor. The last royal pilgrim was Queen Mary in 1563. The pilgrimage remained such a popular one after the

Reformation that Parliament had to suppress the practice by statute towards the end of the sixteenth century. Wigtown was still venerated, however, and Ninian's name continued to be revered.

St Columba

Columba – in Gaelic Columcille, 'dove of the church' – was born around 521 in Donegal, the child of an aristocratic warrior-caste family. According to legend, his mother had a premonition that her son's influence would be great, spreading all over Ireland and beyond.

From early youth, Columba was brought up to a priestly way of life. He was educated by some of the key figures of the Irish church at that time, and studied scripture extensively. He was credited with numerous miracles from a young age, and travelled the country founding monasteries, including one at Derry in 546, when he was only about 25, and at Durrow in 556.

Iona

Columba's reason for leaving his homeland is unclear. He had apparently taken part in the battle of Cuildreimhne after a violation of sanctuary by the king of Ireland in 561; exile preaching the gospel in Scotland may have been part of the punishment to be paid for such belligerence. However, it is more likely that the trip was a self-inflicted penance made more appealing by his own desire to spread Christianity further afield.

In any case, Columba and twelve followers settled on the island of Iona, off the west coast of Mull in the Hebrides. The king of Dalriada in western Scotland was obviously aware of Columba's important connections in Ireland, and gave him the land to build a monastery in 563.

Columba's Work and Legacy

Columba's biographer Adamnan paints a picture of a charismatic man who was dedicated to the training and education of his followers and led a life of great personal austerity. He worked at Iona for two years, consolidating his position through training, organising and prayer, and supervising the building of the monastery before turning his attentions to the wider community.

Thanks to the foundations already laid down by Ninian, Columba was able to turn his attention to the conversion of the pagan Picts in the north and their ruler, King Brude. Columba was a man who believed in direct action, and made his way to Brude's capital near modern-day Inverness, to confront the king directly and challenge him to convert. According to the legend, Brude was not happy to see his visitor approach, and ordered the gates of the city to be locked against him. On reaching the fortifications, Columba asked to be admitted and was

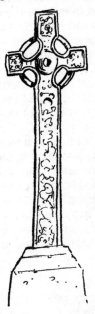

Celtic Cross

refused. Undaunted, the saint simply made the sign of the cross in front of the gates, and they miraculously opened. This and numerous other miracles performed by Columba supposedly convinced the Pictish king and his men to convert to Christianity.

In addition to all his other achievements, Columba was a great scholar. During his career at Iona, he is thought to have transcribed around 300 books. He persuaded Aidan, the Irish King of Dalriada, to be crowned by him in 574. This was the first coronation in Britain with the input of both Church and State, and it set a vitally important precedent, establishing the Church's power to 'make' kings.

Not least among his achievements was that Columba helped complete the jigsaw puzzle of the Christian map of Scotland, and he is still revered today both in Scotland and in Ireland. He was a visionary and a healer, a man of action and of contemplation, and many miracles were associated with him both during his life and after his death. A bone relic of Columba's is thought to be contained in the precious eighth-century box called the Monymusk Reliquary, which is now held in Edinburgh's National Museum of

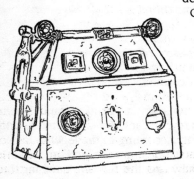

The Monymusk Reliquary

Antiquities. Long revered by the Scots, the Reliquary has been used to bless Scots troops in battle, as it did at Bannockburn in 1314.

Despite its remoteness his monastery swiftly became a popular pilgrimage centre, and centuries after his death in 597, the island of Iona is still revered, with many prominent Scots, including kings and political leaders, buried there. His spirit and example, too, are still carried on in the work of the religious group, the Iona Community. The island's continued prominence fulfils the prediction made by Columba on his deathbed, when he supposedly proclaimed, 'Unto this place, small and mean though it be, great homage shall yet be paid'.

St Mungo

Also known as St Kentigern, Mungo is the patron saint of Glasgow, a city he was closely associated with throughout his life, and one where he did much of his work.

Like his Irish contemporary Columba, Mungo was born into a branch of the royal family around 520 AD. The colourful tale of his conception and birth sets the tone for many of the subsequent stories of miracles in his life.

His mother, St Thenew, whose name was later misinterpreted as St Enoch, was the Christian daughter of a pagan king of Lothian. She was raped and became pregnant, sins for which her irate father sentenced her to death, casting her adrift in a coracle into the Firth of Forth. Fortunately, her craft came to shore at on the north side of the Firth at Culross, near the monastery of St Serf. He looked after both Thenew and the son she gave birth to shortly afterwards, and the pair were baptised there.

St Thenew

Although the life of her son has passed into legend, little is known of the life of Thenew after Munto's birth. She remains one among just a handful of female saints in Scotland, her name, ironically, being best known today from St Enoch's Square in the centre of Glasgow.

The Founding of Glasgow Cathedral

According to the mythology that has sprung up around the life of Mungo over the centuries, he was travelling west when he stopped to speak to a hermit he saw by the road. For the hermit, Fergus, this meeting was the fulfilment of a prophesy told to him that he would not die until he met Mungo. He died thereafter, and Mungo put his body on a cart yoked to two wild bulls. They bore the hermit's body away, stopping at the site of an old cemetery where, at the site of the future Glasgow Cathedral, Fergus was buried.

Mungo himself did not reach the Glasgow area for some time. In 543, he became Bishop of Cumbria, which at that time included parts of southern Scotland. He is said to have travelled to help convert the pagans in Wales, where he met St David. Responding to an invitation from the Christian King of Strathclyde, Mungo moved north again, this time basing himself near the cemetery where Fergus was buried, an area then known as Glesgu, meaning 'dear green place'. Mungo's career there lasted many years, and included a visit from Columba in 584.

Glasgow's Coat of Arms

The coat of arms of the city where Mungo did so much of his work reflects the legends surrounding his life and the many miracles he was believed to have performed.

The bird represents St Serf's pet robin which Mungo miraculously brought back to life. A frozen branch which he made burn in the dead of winter is also shown, together with a bell sent to him by the pope, and a fish with a ring in its mouth.

This last element of the arms symbolises another legendary miracle. The king of Strathclyde was jealous of his wife's relationship with one of his courtiers, and cast into the river her ring which she had given the courtier as a gift. He ordered her to wear the ring or be proved to have been unfaithful, a crime punishable by death. At the queen's request, Mungo advised her that the ring would be found in the mouth of a salmon pulled from the river. One of his monks went out and caught the fish, so saving the queen's life.

St Margaret

The only Scots monarch who has ever been canonised is the saintly Queen Margaret of Scotland (c.1046–93), an important figure in the country's history in her own right as well as an icon of the Church. Her pious work was less dramatic than the miracles of Columba and Mungo, but she was responsible for transforming the lives of many individuals.

Margaret was born into the Anglo-Saxon royal family and was a descendant of King Alfred. Her family had a strong claim to the throne in pre-Conquest days but were forced to spend much time living abroad in Europe, earning her father the name Edward the Exile. Margaret's own upbringing was mostly in Hungary, in an atmosphere of piety and strong Christian belief.

After the Conquest in 1066, life became difficult for those connected with the old regime. The strong claims of Margaret's brother, Edgar Aethling, to the throne, did not endear the family to the new Norman rulers, and they fled north.

Her Marriage and Rule

On their arrival in Scotland, Margaret and her family were met by the Scottish king, Malcolm III, known as Malcolm Canmore (which meant 'Great Head'), who was immediately impressed both by Margaret's beauty and her piety. They were married in 1069 at Dunfermline.

Margaret

Folklore invariably presents the marriage of Malcolm and Margaret as a love match, the perfect fairytale romance of a beauty-and-the-beast pairing: a rough-hewn, older man and a cultured, cultivated and pious young woman. Legends of their mutual love abound, including the story of how Malcolm, unable himself either to read or write, nevertheless bought a religious book for his wife which he then had set in gold and encrusted with precious jewels. However, given their respective positions in society, their match must have been based on more than love at first sight.

For some years, Malcolm had been venturing south of the Border, making raids into English territory. The Normans had forced him to swear to stop these forays, so there would have been obvious appeal in an alliance with the family of Edgar Aethling, the pretender to the English throne.

Margaret does not seem to have been keen on the idea of marriage at first: Malcolm had to ask for her hand on a number of occasions before she finally consented. She seems to have been reluctant to sacrifice her self-denying life of piety, but may have been persuaded by the precarious position of her family. They had just escaped from Norman England, and if Malcolm were to take offence at her rejection, he could easily force them to return. But whatever their true reasons, there is no doubt that the royal couple were a well-matched pair who ruled over a period of prosperity and strength for Scotland.

Margaret has been criticised for bringing practices in both Church and royal court more into line with those in Europe and England, leaving aside the traditional practices of the Church in Scotland and the Gaelic court. But with her changes Margaret improved literacy in Scotland and made the Scottish court something of a cultural centre in Europe. In the Church, too, her introduction of European practices into the flagging Church in Scotland was the catalyst for a wave of monastic foundations across the country. One of her most famous works was the foundation of Dunfermline Priory, and she also had built her own small chapel at Edinburgh Castle.

Her Legends

St Margaret's Hope at the Firth of Forth is supposedly

where the future queen first set foot in Scotland. The name of the towns of North and South Queensferry also commemorate her frequent boat trips between Lothian and Fife to visit her favourite shrine at St Andrews. She also encouraged others to undertake the pilgrimage by granting free ferry trips to all. (The ferry has, of course, long since been replaced by the Forth Rail and Road bridges.)

The most poignant legends surrounding St Margaret are to do with her alms-giving. A woman of great personal and practical piety, she is said to have washed the feet of her poorest subjects and fed orphan children from her own dish. She also personally ransomed the English captives and hostages of her husband's continued raids into Northumberland.

Margaret was also a frequent practitioner of fasting and abstinence, to the detriment of her own health. By her mid-40s, she had fallen ill, her health damaged from the effects of self-imposed frugality as well as the rigours of bearing seven children. She was already seriously ill when she heard the news of the death of her husband and her eldest son on the battlefield, and with her last words she thanked God for the agonising pain of the knowledge so that the sins might be cleansed from her own soul. She died four days later and was buried in Dunfermline Abbey. Three of the seven children of Margaret and Malcolm went on to become kings of Scotland: Edgar, Alexander and David.

Margaret was canonised by Pope Innocent IV in 1251 and remains one of the most popular of Scottish saints. Proof of this can still be seen today, and the saint's name lives on in the many children called Margaret in her honour. Although numbers of parents choosing the name have fallen off since the 1960s, it is still one of the commonest names in Scotland.

St John Ogilvie

After the Reformation in Scotland in the mid-sixteenth century, the Kirk tried to suppress all signs of the old religion, including the cult of the saints. But despite the harsh punishments meted out to discovered recusants, Catholicism continued to be practised and sainthood was still venerated, as the case of John Ogilvie well illustrates.

Born around 1579 into a strict Calvinist family in northeast Scotland, John Ogilvie followed the trend of many young men of his time, going to Europe for much of his education. While he was abroad, he converted to Catholicism and, after studying with the Society of Jesus, himself became a Jesuit. In 1613 he returned to Scotland disguised as a horse-trader, secretly to offer support and services to the country's underground Catholic population. He first returned to the area of his birth, then conducted his secret Masses in Edinburgh and finally in Glasgow. It was there that he was eventually betrayed by Adam Boyd, who came to Ogilvie claiming to want instruction in the Catholic faith, but who was in fact the nephew of the Archbishop of Glasgow.

John Ogilvie was immediately arrested and taken to Edinburgh where he was imprisoned and tortured in an attempt to make him recant and name his accomplices. Despite sleep deprivation and needles pushed under his nails, he refused to do so and was returned to Glasgow for trial. He continued his refusal to accept the authority of the Church of Scotland, and was hanged in February 1615.

Although the official position was against the cult of sainthood, popular opinion was often rather different, and John Ogilvie's principled stand, especially in the face of torture, impressed many. After his death he was hailed as a martyr by other Jesuits, and the papal authorities began gathering information about him for the canonisation process in the 1620s. However, with no official Catholic presence in Scotland, it was 300 years before he was beatified – an important stage on the official journey to sainthood.

A number of miraculous cures were attributed to his intercession, but it was the curing of a Glasgow man, John Fagin, from a state of near-death from terminal cancer, that finally led to John Ogilvie's canonisation in 1976.

◆ After the Reformation ◆ ◆

Throughout the period after the Reformation and usually in the face of official-Church disapproval, Scotland's saints continued to be venerated by both Catholic and Protestant believers. But the strength and vibrancy of the cults of Scottish saints do not apply only to the martyrs and legendary figures who died many centuries ago. Even today, many Catholics in Scotland and beyond are campaigning for the canonisation of Margaret Sinclair.

Margaret Sinclair

Born in 1900 in Edinburgh, Margaret was the third of six children, and by all accounts was extremely devout in her religious beliefs and practices from early childhood. In her early twenties she decided to become a nun, joining the austere order of the Poor Clares in London. But early on in 1925, Margaret contracted tuberculosis, and despite the severity and discomfort of her illness, she continued to display the same serenity and devotion that so impressed many of those who met her. She died in November 1925 and her body was returned to Edinburgh for burial.

Soon after her death, miraculous cures began to be attributed to Margaret Sinclair's intercession and she became known locally as Edinburgh's 'Wonder Worker'. In 1978, she was declared Venerable by Pope Paul VI, on the grounds that she 'possessed the theological virtues of Faith, Hope and Charity towards God and her neighbour, and the cardinal virtues Prudence, Justice, Temperance and Fortitude ... to a heroic degree'. Compared to the swashbuckling and action-packed legends surrounding many of Scotland's older saints, the life of Blessed Margaret Sinclair seems somewhat unspectacular. Yet the movement to bring about her canonisation is proof of the continuing devotion in modern-day Scotland to saints and the idea of sainthood.

10: *Plants*

Plants, trees and herbs have each in their own way been at the foundations of the development of life in Scotland since the last Ice Age. From the use of herbs and plants for food, through wood for building materials, peat and wood for heating and cooking and a largely plant-based diet, they have helped provide the essentials of life in Scotland's harsh climate. Plants were also used for dyeing wool and fabrics and were, of course, the only treatment for most ills.

The life cycle of plants was central to the beliefs of the pagan Celts. The natural order of birth, death and rebirth throughout the seasons was at the core of the teachings and rituals of the Druids, leaders of the dominant pre-Christian sect in Scotland.

With such a key role in the establishment and maintenance of life in the country, and in the beliefs and practices of its people, it is not surprising that a whole mythology of its own has grown up around Scotland's indigenous plant life.

◆ The Thistle ◆ ◆

The plant that is most readily associated with Scotland is the thistle. The legend of the thistle's adoption as the emblem of the nation dates back almost a thousand years to the era of the Vikings and the Scandinavian domination of the Scottish islands.

A Norse attack on the north-easternmost corner of the country compelled King Kenneth III (997–1005) to ride north to repel a threatened wholesale invasion. The king set up his camp for the night not far from where the invaders were thought to be planning a landing, but unbeknown to the sleeping Scots the Vikings crept ashore under the cover of darkness, until they were almost upon the Scots' camp.

But as the invaders were closing in, one of them stepped on a thistle. His involuntary cry of shock and pain was heard by the Scots' sentries, who roused the camp and fought off the invaders. The legend goes that Kenneth III was so grateful that he adopted the thistle as his nation's emblem.

The Symbol of Scotland

The thistle's place as the national symbol was recognised officially by its appearance on the national coinage from the reign of James III in 1470. By 1503, when James IV married Margaret Tudor, it was certainly a well-used emblem of Scotland and its royal family, and the union of the Scots and English royal houses that year was commemorated in the allegorical poem *The Thrissil and the Rois*, a celebration of the marriage by William Dunbar, James' court poet.

National Motto

Over the years the prickly plant has also been compared to the idea – albeit a stereotypical one – of the Scottish temperament. The motto ascribed to the plant has also been adopted unofficially by the country it has come to represent. 'Nemo me impune lacessit' was the motto of the Order of the Thistle, the ancient Scots order of chivalry. The motto of both plant and order usually translates in Scots as 'Wha daur meddle wi' me' or, in the more prosaic English translation, 'No-one interferes with me with impunity' – a motto thought to apply equally well both to the plant and to the people of the nation it represents. The motto is still used in the same context today and is most commonly seen stamped on the edges of Scottish pound coins.

◆ *Heather* ◆ ◆

Another plant that has come to be strongly associated with Scotland is heather. While the thistle was the nation's symbolic emblem, heather was the omnipresent, every-use workhorse of Scottish plant life. But despite its associations, few people realise that widespread heather growth is actually a sign of an over-grazed and damaged landscape. Yet heather remains an extremely useful and versatile plant which at one time could be found almost anywhere in a Scottish home: walls, thatch, bedding, fire, floor, ale, tea, baskets, medicines, dye, brushes and cattle feed – all these were either made of heather, or else contained it. Heather rope was even found in the Neolithic settlement of Skara Brae in Orkney, which dates back around 4000 years, while other excavations suggest the use of heather as bedding material in Iron Age settlements.

Lucky Charm

Heather is widely available and still very popular in Scotland today. Rarer than the purple variety is white heather, believed to bring its

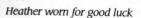

Heather worn for good luck

bearer good luck and still worn as a good-luck charm and ornament, pinned to jacket lapels. This belief may have arisen from the myth that beds of white heather were the resting places of good fairies.

◆ Plantlore ◆ ◆

Much of the belief in Scottish plantlore is based on the power to heal or to harm inherent in various plants. Different plants were used to treat a huge range of conditions and illnesses, from heart trouble and epilepsy to insect bites and skin rashes.

It is difficult to work out precisely how some of these herbal remedies worked, so completely has modern science and medicine taken the place of the traditional approach to healing. In spite of their undoubted efficacy, herbal treatments very quickly became much less popular as modern medicine appeared to offer all the answers.

But the closing years of the twentieth century have heralded a counter-swing in attitude, as the limitations of antibiotic-based medicine become increasingly obvious. Many people, including some practitioners of conventional medicine, have moved back towards this holistic approach to health and healing, especially as so many of the traditional remedies, for years dismissed as old wives' tales, have been scientifically scrutinised and tested, and been proved effective.

Plants for Medicine

Herbs and plants were used in different forms. Some were mixed with water to produce potions and infusions, while others were powdered and sewn into sachets to be carried as charms. Until the late Middle Ages, around the fifteenth century, all medical practitioners were basically herbalists.

In a world with neither anaesthetic nor analgesic to provide either sleep or pain relief, the arts of the healer were essential to the well-being of their community. Herbs were their vital tool and, like all other plants, some had better associations than others; for example, thyme was thought to be a fairy favourite.

Traditional healers were operational at the same point in the Middle Ages when what is now known as conventional medicine began to develop in Scotland, as access to universities became possible in the 1400s. From the beginning, scientific and academic medicine was practised almost exclusively by men. They travelled to the great European universities to be educated, then returned to practice in Scottish towns and cities. This contrasts with the mainly female healers who continued to be dominant in rural communities. Mutual distrust was very strong, even though many of the treatments being dispensed by the two groups were virtually identical in content. A fifteenth-century text used by Scottish physicians recommended the use of willow sap to control bleeding, a traditional folk remedy that would have been practised by herbal healers for centuries.

Plants for Witchcraft

The anti-witch hysteria that gripped large parts of Scotland in the seventeenth century was very dangerous for traditional healers (see ch. 6). Anyone perceived as being different from society's norms was a potential target – no-one moreso that the local wise-woman with her closely guarded and esoteric knowledge of herbs and plantlore. Such knowledge of plants and herbs was known as 'wort cunning'.

Obviously, wort cunning had the potential to be used for ill as well as for good, and many healers undoubtedly satisfied a local demand for love potions, fortune-telling and other minor transgressions of the rulings against dabbling in the 'black arts'. A much smaller number altogether may have tried to involve themselves in darker practices.

During the witch-hunts, uncounted numbers of Scotland's innocent folk healers fell victim and no doubt many more were too afraid of the consequences to practice. As a consequence, whole areas of the country were left without a healer. Although folk medicine did survive this period, it was never as widespread again, and never recovered its previous status.

Plants as Witches' Poisons

The plants and herbs most usually associated with witches were those with the power to harm. Monk's Head, also known as 'Wolf's Bane', was a well-known example – it produced the powerful poison aconite.

Henbane, used for pain relief or as an anaesthetic, was a potent and poisonous plant that could also be used in magic. An excavation at the site of a medieval monastery in East Lothian uncovered a great concentration of henbane and some hemlock seeds at the site of the monks' hospital.

Hemlock, one of the most famous of witches' medicines, was available in Scottish gardens, especially in the south and east of the country where it flourished; it was both poisonous and hallucinogenic. It also worked as a sedative, and was used in the treatment of spasms and epilepsy.

Another notorious poison associated with witches was Deadly Nightshade, also known as Belladonna. Although it is an extremely poisonous and narcotic plant, it was relatively rare in Scotland: it is a member of the same family as henbane, which was more commonly found.

Plants for Other Uses

Blackberry bushes were also known as brambles in Scotland. They had many uses – as a dye, as a medicine and to protect against supernatural influences. For this reason, bramble hedges were especially popular, and often grown around fields of crops or cattle where they performed a double duty, protecting the animals from evil spirits and also providing a sturdy barrier to prevent them from straying.

St John's Wort is another plant credited with strong protective properties against evil spirits or the evil eye, and it is closely associated with St Columba. One of its Gaelic names translates as 'armpit package of Columba' due to the saint's habit of carrying the plant tucked under his arm. This may have been due to his belief in its protection – against evil, rather than perspiration – but it is more likely that he was using it as a poultice, placed where it could most easily be absorbed. It was used, among other things, as a treatment for worms, as a diuretic and to help improve the blood. But recognition of its powers far predates Christianity, as it was used in pagan midsummer festivals and may have been used to light Beltane bon-fires. Its golden flowers made it attractive to the Druids as a sun symbol.

The same is true of the daisy, and indeed the practice of hanging daisy chains around the necks of young children – still done today in fun – was intended to protect them from malign forces.

Modern-day uses

Some Scottish folk remedies are still practised and popular. One which is still widely found is the use of common dock leaves rubbed on inflamed skin as an antidote to nettle stings. It is also commonly held that wherever nettles are growing, a dock plant will be found growing close by.

Another old belief that retains popularity is in the power of a four-leaf clover. This relatively rare plant was thought to offer protection against evil fairies and is still believed by many to bring good luck. Like much in luck and magic, however, it must be acquired as a free gift, as it is only effective if found by accident. If it is deliberately sought out, the plant will be useless to its finder.

Flowers

Flowers are important in a variety of rituals, and have been for many centuries. Floral tributes after death, and the placing of flowers on a grave, are pagan practices, where the floral wreaths may have represented the unending cycle of life and death. Individual blooms were held to represent particular qualities or properties. Flowers are also carried and worn at weddings, and traditionally the type of blooms chosen depended on their particular symbolism, but now the bride is more likely to chose her personal favourites, or something to match the colours of her outfit.

A common superstition relating to flowers can still be found in Scotland. It was believed to be extremely bad luck to put red and white flowers in a vase together, and until recently nurses would not allow red and white bouquets to be displayed in hospital wards.

Roses

Roses, and especially rosehips, were widely used in folk medicine, especially to treat digestive problems. They are also traditional ingredients for wine, tea and jam, and provided an excellent source of vitamin C. They were widely used in cooking until the mid twentieth century (and still feature in children's medicine).

A white rose is a symbol of the Stuarts, the Scottish royal family, and the flower was traditionally worn by Jacobites on 10 June, the birthday of Prince Charles Edward Stuart, Bonnie Prince Charlie.

Orchids

The wild orchids found growing in many areas of the country were carried as love talismans after they had been dried, and as a means of predicting in love. If the powdered root was placed beneath the pillow, it would induce dreams of the future spouse. It could also be used as a love potion. If the desired person could be made to eat some of it unknowingly, they would fall in love with the person who had fed it to them. As usual, however, it was a double-edged sword, and care and expertise was called for– if the wrong part of the root was used, it would induce repulsion in the eater instead.

Bluebells

Abundant in woods throughout Scotland, the bluebell is seen as a sign of the arrival of spring. Bluebell woods were regarded with awe as places of great enchantment and were believed to be places where fairies lived. For those brave or foolhardy enough to venture in, hearing the

Bluebells

bluebells ring was a sign of their own impending death.

Dandelions

The dandelion is a very common plant in Scotland and was put to many uses. Its roots and leaves were made into wine or tea, or used in a tonic for their diuretic and stimulant properties. So powerful were these that they gave the plant its common names of 'piss-a-bed' or the more modern 'pee-the-bed' – the latter, now a child's term of abuse, is used for reasons undoubtedly long since forgotten.

In a reference to another of its useful functions, the dandelion was also called 'doon-head clock' after it had flowered, when its downy head could supposedly be used to tell the time by being blown away. The number of puffs required was supposed to represent the hour of day.

Fungi

The damp Scottish countryside is home to a range of wild mushrooms and toadstools. Some of these, so-called 'magic mushrooms', have been picked and eaten from the time of the Druids for their hallucinogenic powers. Toadstools were associated with the fairies, and a circle of toadstools was believed to be evidence of fairy activity.

◆ Trees ◆ ◆

Symbols of strength and protection, trees were revered by the Druids and the ancient Celtic peoples. Each one was thought to have a spirit which could physically manifest itself, like the dryads of ancient Greek legend, and it was common for people to apologise to the spirit before cutting wood from the tree. Some trees were considered particularly powerful, although the Celts believed that all should be respected.

Reverence for the tree continued on into Christian times, since when it was regarded as particularly venerable as the object on which Christ had been crucified, although there has been some argument over exactly which tree was used (see p. 231).

Even in modern times, trees are still important symbols

in Scotland, and it is common to plant a special tree to commemorate a particular event or a person who has died.

Rowan

Pride of place among all the plants that feature in Scottish folklore must go to the rowan tree, or mountain ash. Credited with powerful properties, it was thought capable of deflecting any type of malign influence, from the evil eye and spells, through diseases to fairies.

The rowan was incorporated into Scottish homes in all sorts of ways to bestow its pro-tective properties. Wherever possible, the cross-beam of the house's chimney would be made of the wood of the rowan tree. Or, if it was not practical to do this, a rowan twig would be nailed to the house lintel or pinned in a cross-shape above the mantelpiece. Many Highland homes traditionally had a rowan tree growing in their front garden.

Rowan wood was also used wherever possible around the home. Items as diverse as but-ter churns, carts, ploughs, spinning wheels – anything

A rowan cross

that could be interfered with or damaged by fairies, or have its contents affected by malign magic would ideally be made of it to avert evil influence.

Rowan was not just a powerful charm for humans; it could also be used to protect animals. Like their human counterparts, those animals who were about to give birth were considered to be most at risk from bad influences, and a necklace of rowan berries would often be hung around the creatures' necks to protect both the mother and her young from harm. A sprig of rowan could also be tied onto a horse's or cow's tail, usually with red thread or ribbon which had been dyed using the berries of the tree. Red was considered to be a particularly effective colour against fairies as it is the colour of blood and so represented life. The bright red berries of the rowan tree must also have been an important factor in its achieving such a high status.

A story from the island of Arran tells of a young farmer who was taking a cow to market when he removed the sprig of rowan tied to the animal's tail. The cow promptly lay down in the road and refused to move until a woman living nearby threw a handy bucket of urine over it! Understandably, the cow decided to move and ran straight back to the farm. The next day, the farmer re-attached the rowan sprig and succeeded in getting the animal to the market.

Elder

The elder tree was also the subject of strong beliefs; these tended to vary from district to district across the country. In some areas, to bring elder wood into the home was to tempt bad luck, and to burn the wood of an elder tree was to bring in the Devil.

According to different legends, elder was either the tree on which Christ was crucified (although this seems very unlikely, given its slender, twisting branches) or else it was the tree on which Judas Iscariot hanged himself. Other tales claim Christ's cross was, in fact, made of aspen.

Some ancient legends claim that elders were hiding places for witches, whose spirits would take up residence within the wood of the tree. Because of this, it was important that elder should not be used to make household items such as cradles, bowls and tools.

One way of discovering who had been casting spells and practising witchcraft was to chop a branch off a nearby elder tree. If someone from the neighbourhood then appeared with a bad cut to their hand or arm, they were held to be witches, whose spirit had been residing in the elder tree.

Conflicting Myths

Despite such strongly negative associations, the elder was also at the centre of a series of counter-myths which, unusually, stressed properties which were quite the opposite. These legends claimed that the tree was actually one of the most potent against witchcraft, when used as rowan was: for example, an elder cross would be hung on the door of a barn or stable to guard the crops or animals inside.

But whether or not people associated the tree with the black arts, it was widely acknowledged to be among the most useful and beneficial in one particular respect: its healing properties were second to none, with almost every part of the plant having some medicinal purpose or other. The leaves were made into an ointment for application to bruises, chilblains or headaches; the berries were infused or made into a paste to treat rheumatism, syphilis, epilepsy and piles, while elderberry wine made a palatable treatment for colds, asthma and sciatica. The elder was also a key ingredient in many dyes, as its various parts produced a range of colours, including purple from the berries, yellow from the leaves and black from the bark, and it was used in the production of Harris tweed.

Willow

The willow is thought to have been one of the first trees to grow again in Scotland after the end of the Ice Age. It was a versatile tree, whose wood was used by diverse trades, from carpentry and furniture-making to healing. Less prosaically, its versatility did not prevent the willow's being attributed with magical properties, and it was commonly used in Druidic ceremonial.

The pain-killing effects of willow are well known: its bark contains one of the key ingredients used in aspirin. In the Highlands, children's teething rings were made of aspen, a member of the willow family. Explanations for the use of the wood in this way stated that aspen may have been the wood used for Christ's crucifixion and so the wood of the ring would protect children from evil. However, a more likely explanation is that the wood's analgesic properties meant that chewing on it would have dulled the teething pains for the child.

'Wicca', the name still used today for good, or white, witchcraft, was supposedly derived from the use of willow to make wicker effigies for ceremonial sacrifices and Beltane fires.

Oak

Oak was another tree which was particularly associated with the Druids, and it was revered by the Celtic peoples throughout Europe. It was not uncommon for chief druids and ancient kings to be buried in the hollowed-out trunk of an oak tree. Although in Scotland the oak was less highly regarded than rowan, it was still considered very powerful. Oak wood was used for fires at the midsummer and midwinter solstice festivals, and in Beltane rites. Its pagan connection with fire may have stemmed from its immense size, as oak trees would often have been struck by lightning in a landscape where they were by far the tallest feature.

This association of oak with strongly rooted pagan beliefs was used, adapted and built on by the early Christian Church. Oak groves had been traditional places of ancient worship, and many of the first Scottish Christian churches were sited in them: on the island of Iona, a key location of early Scottish Christianity, St Columba's chapel was built of oak.

Mistletoe

Although, strictly speaking, a shrub rather than a tree, mistletoe is a plant which is associated with the oak – on which it often grows as a parasite – and is particularly well-known for its association with Druids. As an ever-green it was highly valued, and the Druids respected its powers so much that it was ceremoniously harvested for their rituals using a gold sickle.

But mistletoe's powerful properties were also widely appreciated beyond the hallowed Druidical circle. The plant's Gaelic name is *uile-ice*, meaning 'all heal' and it was, not surprisingly, used to treat a great variety of serious ailments, including heart problems, abscesses and epilepsy. Some accounts of nineteenth-century healers in Inverness show that they prescribed mistletoe tea for the treatment of palpitations.

Hazel

Hazel is another tree associated with many old Scottish beliefs. It was sacred to the ancient Celtic fire god Thunor (the equivalent of Thor) because it was the best wood for making fire by friction.

Hazelnuts were also believed to bestow powers of creativity and fertility, both literally and metaphorically. They were believed to improve human fertility, while the Druids believed that eating them could not only confer the gift of prophesy, but also that they bestowed on bards their knowledge of epic legends and ability to write songs and poems.

A walking stick made from hazel would give protection to travellers against any evil spirits they could encounter, and in the hands of a magician or wizard, it could even make its carrier invisible. The staffs of Druids were made of hazel and, in deference to the powers of the plant and its lore, so were those of the early Christian bishops. It was also the preferred wood for divination of water, and hazel rods were used to help detect veins of coal and other minerals.

Ash

Ash was a popular and useful tree and was often cut to make switches for cattle. It also featured strongly in Druidical rites: its wood was used to make Yule logs, and the hallucinogenic properties of its roots were highly valued by the Druids for their ability to induce visions, especially at midsummer when the tree was at its most vigorous and powerful.

Beech

The beech was also thought to be significant – it was a symbol of remembrance. Legends tell of the seven beeches planted by Jacobite sympathisers at Glen Moidart in Inverness, in memory of the 'Seven Men of Moidart' who landed at Loch-nan-Uamh with Prince Charles Edward Stuart, Bonnie Prince Charlie, in 1745.

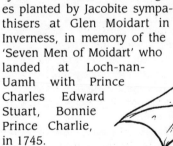

Holly

A hardy plant that can adapt well to harsh condi-

Berried holly

tions, holly grows all over Scotland. Its presence was encouraged in many areas, as it was thought to offer protection against the evil eye and it was used, like the bramble, to form protective hedges and restrain livestock. Like another potent plant, the rowan, holly's red berries make it more powerful, as they symbolise life. The holly is also an evergreen plant, and its ability to withstand the most extreme weather conditions unaffected has probably added to its legendary status.

COLLINS

COLLINS POCKET REFERENCE